GOD'S WILL
for
YOU

Discovering your Destiny through Discipleship

MICAH LANE

CROSSBOOKS

CrossBooks™
A Division of LifeWay
1663 Liberty Drive
Bloomington, IN 47403
www.crossbooks.com
Phone: 1-866-879-0502

Scripture taken from the New King James Version. Copyright 1979, 1980,
1982 by Thomas Nelson, inc. Used by permission. All rights reserved.

First published by CrossBooks 6/20/2014

ISBN: 978-1-4627-3832-8 (sc)
ISBN: 978-1-4627-3833-5 (hc)
ISBN: 978-1-4627-3831-1 (e)

Library of Congress Control Number: 2014910563

Printed in the United States of America.

This book is printed on acid-free paper.

In Honor of Father,
Rev. Elton A. Lane,
"The Real Preacher Lane"
who always taught us
God's Will is best.

And

To
Lyn, Austin, Aaron, and Megan
content to walk with me
in
the Will of God

CONTENTS

PREFACE

The hype was astounding. Headlines in local newspapers, billboards along the highway that led to this coastal getaway, and promotional segments on the evening news inundated the minds of vacationers, as well as the locals. Word spread far and wide that the new theme park was going to be the hottest new attraction on the strand. The vision of multitudes filling the park each day for concerts, rides, food and fun motivated investors. It had purpose, promise, and lots of potential. It seemed the dream would come true and millions upon millions of dollars would be made annually.

Opening day did not disappoint. With great pomp and circumstance the park was unveiled with several famous rock bands of yesteryear and a skyline decorated with fireworks.

The glory, however, quickly faded. The economy tanked. The crowds grew smaller and smaller. Within a year the gates closed and the owners filed for bankruptcy. Everything came to a sudden halt. The noise that once kept the neighbors awake at night had fallen silent. The dream became a nightmare.

Presently, nothing happens. The Rock bands left the premises long ago and the featured coaster just stands idle in the sun and wind without any real purpose. Grass is pushing through the asphalt in the empty parking lots that surround the 140-acre park. It made the perfect setting for the filming of a recent episode of a doomsday drama depicting an abandoned, forgotten, former centra of entertainment. Questions circulated among businessmen for months, even years, about the possibilities of reinvestment or resurrection. Any hope of making something out of what has been dubbed by the industry as a "cataclysmic failure?"

Tragically, thousands of people think of their own lives in the same way. Life has let them down. They feel like complete failures. They have all but lost hope of fulfilling their dreams. Some are wondering if they will accomplish any of their goals and they feel as if they are losing precious time with each passing day. Perhaps, you, too, wonder if your life can get back on course. Is there hope of resurrecting your dreams? Is it too late?

There is hope for you and every person through a personal relationship with Jesus Christ. God has a purpose and a plan for your life. This work in your hands is designed to help you discover your destiny. It's not too late. God is still reaching out to you to show you the wonderful agenda that He designed for you long before you were ever born.

Myriads of people are searching for answers about life. Among Christians, some of the most frequently asked questions center on God's will. Many of God's children, young and old, are asking, "What does God want me to do with my life?" They desire to know what purpose they have for existence.

No matter who you are, God certainly has a plan and a purpose for your life. He loves you with an everlasting love. He sent His Son, Jesus Christ, to die on a cross to save you from sin, and to give you life, peace, purpose, and hope (John 3:16; Rom 5:1-5). I love the promise of God made to His people through the prophet Jeremiah: "For I know the thoughts that I think toward you, says the Lord, thoughts of peace and not of evil, to give you a future and a hope. Then you will call upon Me and go and pray to Me, and I will listen to you. And you will seek Me and find Me, when you search for Me with all your heart" (Jeremiah 29:11-13).

God has a plan for your life and He is willing to reveal that plan to you and help you fulfill it to His glory. May God give you wisdom as you seek to discover and do His will.

INTRODUCTION

It's All About Redemption

"In Him we have redemption through His blood, the forgiveness of sins, according to the riches of His grace." *Ephesians 1:7*

Our son Austin is an accomplished artist. Before he begins to sketch or paint, the paper positioned before him is totally blank. The process begins with the imagination. The mental picture precedes the literal. He envisions what he wants the artistic creation to look like at the finish. He crafts his work one step at a time. He begins with a basic sketch and adds detail in progression until he completes the work of art.

If you are a Christian you should know that God has a purpose and a plan for your life. God has a master plan that we all fit into. As we grow in our relationship with God and seek to discover and do His will we must never lose sight of the big picture of the work of God that is revealed in the Bible. In a word, the big picture of what God is doing in the world is "Redemption." Boyd Hunt explains: "Redemption is the Bible's key concept. The term summarizes in a single word the entire biblical message. Given the standpoint of biblical revelation, the triune creator God is, above all else, Redeemer."[1]

W.A. Criswell once preached a series of sermons entitled "The Scarlet Thread of Redemption" in which he traced the theme of redemption through every book of the Bible from Genesis to Revelation.[2] All that God is doing in the lives of believers today has something to do with redemption. God loves all people and desires to set them free from the bondage of sin (John 8:31-32). He has redeemed us and given us purpose in life. God has "reconciled us to Himself and given to us the ministry of reconciliation" (2 Cor 5:18-20). He is still working to bring lost people into a personal relationship with Himself.

Keeping the big picture of "Redemption" in mind is so critical to understanding what God desires to accomplish in the lives of His beloved children. He does everything with a redemptive purpose. Mankind is lost and in need of Salvation (Rom 3:23). God is at work in His own creation to redeem it and to bring glory to Himself. Jesus Christ, the Son of God is the redeemer (Gal 4:5-6). He is the central figure in God's great redemptive story. Vern S. Polythress makes this point in his contribution in the book, *Understanding the Big Picture of the Bible*: "The work of Christ on earth, and especially his crucifixion and resurrection, is the climax of history; it is the great turning point at which God actually accomplished the salvation toward which history had been moving throughout the Old Testament. The present era looks back on Christ's completed work but also looks forward to the consummation of his work when Christ will come again and when there will appear "new heavens and a new earth in which righteousness dwells" (2 Pet 3:13).[3]

Every believer fits perfectly into God's all important plan. He has redeemed us who believe in His own Son to work through us that others might believe and be redeemed also. The big picture of God's redemption will help believers better understand the specific details of God's personal plan for their lives. I do not know the specific details of God's personal will for you but I know for certain that God desires for all to be saved (1 Tim 2:1). It is also clear that God desires for all who are saved to be shaped into the image of His Son (Rom 8:29). It's all about redemption. Without a doubt, this is God's will for you.

The heart of God's great redemptive work is taught by the apostle Paul in Ephesians 2:8-10. The essence of the work that God is doing in mankind to accomplish His divine purpose in the world can be broken down into three fundamental concepts: (1) Salvation, a work that Christ has done for us, (2) Sanctification, a work that God does within us, and (3) Special service, a unique work of service that God does through us to bring glory to Himself. A brief overview of these concepts will prepare our minds for discovery.

Salvation

The Bible says that believers in Jesus Christ have been saved. "Saved" speaks of a rescue from imminent peril or great danger. Sin endangers every soul. Without a personal relationship with Christ, a lost man's destiny is eternal separation from God. Therefore, all men need to be saved. God is willing to forgive, cleanse, and redeem anyone who will believe in His Son. The Bible says that salvation comes "by grace" and "through faith" in Jesus Christ (Eph 2:8). Grace means "gift." We are saved by God's unmerited favor. We all deserve separation, condemnation, death, and hell. Instead, because of His unconditional love, mercy, and grace, God has given believers eternal life. Lost sinners receive God's eternal gift of life the moment they trust in the death of Christ as payment for their sins. The crux of the matter is "faith." "The Just shall live by faith" (Rom 1:17). It is "not of works"(Eph 2:9a). The work was completed by our Lord on the cross over two thousand years ago. The debt has been paid in full. If you are not a Christian, you can place your faith in Him now. He will save you. You have no work that needs to be done in order to be redeemed. You need only to repent of sin and trust in Christ.

It's a matter of believing. Faith is the hand that receives God's free gift of salvation.

We are saved to bring glory to Jesus our Savior - "no one should boast" (Eph 2:9b). There is nothing to boast about except the cross (Gal 6:14). Christ is completely responsible for His work of redemption and should be given all of the glory! God has saved us from sin and continues to build character in our lives that we may glorify Him. In fact, "you are saved"(Eph 2:8) is the translation of a perfect tense in Greek. It points to a decisive experience in the past, but it also stresses continual development in the present.[4] The Spirit of Christ indwells every believer to keep shaping them into His likeness. Trusting Christ as Savior is only the beginning of an exciting journey with God.

Sanctification

God continues to work in believers after they have been justified or saved. A believer is a work in progress. "We are God's workmanship" (Eph 2:10). The word "workmanship" refers to a work of art or a masterpiece. Our English word poem is derived from it. You are like a poem, a masterpiece, a work of art is the Master's hands to be perfected before Him. Our redemption is settled but it is not yet complete. God is still shaping us into the persons He has designed us to become.

This is another important aspect of redemption. God wants believers to become more like His Son. He works to fashion us into the image of Christ (Rom 8:28-29). Believers are the handiwork of God until Jesus Christ comes back again. We all have different spiritual gifts, and a diversity of ministries in the body of Christ, but all are called to be saved and become more like Jesus. No matter where we go in the will of God and no matter what we do, the purpose of God, our redeemer, is to make us like Christ by the power of His Spirit.

Something Special

As Christians we have been redeemed for a special purpose in life. God has saved us "unto good works which God prepared beforehand that we should walk in them" (Eph 2:10c). Every believer is called to do something special in Christ's Kingdom. God's new creatures are characterized by "good works." These special works are not the basis of salvation but as a result of salvation. We are not saved by our good works, but we are saved "unto" good works. God has a purpose for every person who calls upon the name of His Son. He has a work for you to fulfill as part of His great redemptive plan.

Our Special Works of Service are to be "Good" (Eph 2:10b). Every person who is a new creation through a personal relationship with Christ should do "good works." For any work to be a good work it must be from God because no one is good but God. The only way a Christian can actually perform any "good" thing is through the power of the indwelling Holy Spirit. God has made us new creatures by His Holy Spirit (Titus 3:5). He continues to work *in* us by His Spirit (Phil 2:12-13). And He works *through* us by His Spirit. All of the "good" of the Christian life is dependent upon the power of the indwelling Christ who strengthens us to do His will (Phil 4:13). As God's handiwork, we should be "doing the will of God from the heart" (Eph 6:6).

Our Special works of Service are "previously prepared" (Eph 2:10c). God already knows the plan that He has for you: " I know the plans that I have for you, saith the Lord. Plans for welfare and not for calamity, to give you a future and a hope (Jeremiah 29:11).

All of the will of God is prepared in advance for followers of Christ. We may not know all of the specific details of His perfect will for us, but God does. He is omniscient. The all-knowing and all-powerful God has already prepared a life work for His children. It is ready for discovery and fulfillment. Currently, in Myrtle Beach, we are waiting on a new overpass to be completed very near our church. None can travel that road until it is completed. No one has access to that path until it is finished. God's will does not require construction. The plan and the path were established long ago. The road has already been paved. We only need to get on God's predetermined path for our lives and follow it. God's path for our lives will lead to the place we need to go. We may not always see clearly where it leads but the path and destination has already been determined.

Our Special works of service are for daily living and serving to the glory of God (Eph 2:10d). We are trophies of God's grace. Living for Jesus and serving Him brings glory to God. This is the big picture: God wants to work in us to shape us into the image of His Son and He wants us to serve and work so that other will see what God is doing in us and desire to walk in His will also. Jesus said, "Let your light so shine before men that they may see your good works and bring glory to My Father in heaven" (Matt 5:16). Give God glory in all things. This is God's will for you.

CHAPTER 1

SALVATION: THE BEGINNING OF GOD'S WILL

"For this is good and acceptable in the sight of God our Savior who desires all men to be saved and to come to the knowledge of the truth." 1 Timothy 2:3-4

Our eight-year-old daughter, Megan, came home from one day school with a little potted plant. She was very proud of what she had accomplished. The sprouts were bursting from the soil with bright-green leaves that soaked up rays of sunshine. She informed me that we must water the plant daily, but just enough to keep the soil moist, so it would continue to grow.

Unaware that my little girl had been blessed with a green thumb, I asked her to tell me how she had succeeded in getting that little plant to grow so beautifully. "It was easy, Dad," she told me. "The teacher brought these little pieces from a bigger plant, and we just put them in this dirt that we got from a bag. And then, well, we just watered them, and these are what we got."

Like my daughter's plant, every beautiful, living, and growing thing has a beginning. God's will begins with a personal relationship with His Son, Jesus Christ. True spiritual life is born when the seed of the gospel is planted and cultivated in the good soil of a believing human heart. It is God's will that lost mankind be reconciled to Him because He wants to fellowship with the people He created.

We have already learned that God is the God of redemption. Salvation, or more specifically justification, is the beginning point in the life of every person who desires to do what pleases God. Human beings can't grow in the knowledge, purpose, and will of God if they don't know Him.

People without Christ are "dead in trespasses and sins" (Eph. 2:1) and unfit for the Master's use. But God makes men useful by transforming their lives through the power of the gospel of Jesus Christ (Rom. 1:16). God works His will in the lives of those who come to Him through faith in His Son. Jesus transforms the sinner into a "new creation" (2 Cor. 5:17).

As believers daily trust, obey, and saturate their minds with the truth of the Word, they continue to mature and grow into the beautiful people whom God intends for them to be. It begins the moment a person becomes a Christian.

The apostle Paul, in his first epistle to Timothy, made it clear that God desires all people to be saved. "For this is good and acceptable in the sight of God our Savior, who desires all men to be saved and to come to the knowledge of the truth. For there is one God and one mediator between God and men, the Man Christ Jesus, who gave Himself a ransom for all, to be testified in due time, for which I was appointed a preacher and an apostle—I am speaking the truth in Christ and not lying—a teacher of the Gentiles in faith and truth" (1 Tim. 2:3–7).

From this passage of Scripture, let us consider the following four wonderful truths about God's work of salvation:

God desires for all people to be saved (v 4).

God's heart is to redeem lost mankind. God wants or desires all men to be delivered from sin and eternal death (v 4). He doesn't want people to spend eternity separated from Him in hell but instead in heaven with Him.

Jesus also plainly stated the will of God the Father concerning sinners: "And this is the will of Him who sent Me, that everyone who sees the Son and believes in Him may have everlasting life; and I will raise him up on the last day" (John 6:40).

The apostle Peter taught the same truth: "The Lord is not slack concerning His promise, as some count slackness, but is longsuffering toward us, not willing that any should perish, but that all should come to repentance" (2 Peter 3:9).

It is God's will that lost sinners be saved, but this doesn't mean that all men and women will be saved. No one should read the doctrine of universalism into this or any Scripture passage. The Bible teaches that "all have sinned and fallen short of God's glory" (Rom. 3:23).

Some will refuse God's offer of salvation and be lost without Him for eternity. This is tragic in light of all that God has done through Christ to redeem lost mankind. God's heart for fallen men is stated clearly in the gospel of John: "For God so loved the world that He gave His only begotten Son that whosoever believes in Him will not perish but have everlasting life"(John 3:16).

A young man desires to marry a sweet and pretty young lady not because he is obligated to marry her, but because he loves her and wants to marry her. In the same way, God wants every person to be saved because He loves every person. He desires an intimate and personal relationship with everyone, having created man to fellowship with Him.

The intimacy of this relationship is demonstrated by the words "in Christ." Paul used this phrase more than seventy times in his epistles. Every redemptive movement of God in our lives comes through our fellowship with Jesus Christ. God's will is found and fulfilled in Christ. Paul states: "In everything give thanks; for this is the will of God in Christ Jesus for you" (1 Thess. 5:18).

God's Son died for all people that they may be saved (vv 5–6).

The God of love sent His Son to die for all that all may be saved (John 3:16). How do we know that God really wants to save sinners? We know because God sent His Son to die for them (Rom 5:8). Jesus, God's Son, came to earth and lived a sinless life. He was crucified, buried, and raised from the dead by the power of the Holy Spirit to give eternal life to all who believe.

Christ is the only Savior, and Paul states that Jesus Christ is the one and only mediator (v 5). A mediator is someone who intervenes between two people either to make or to restore peace and friendship. A husband and wife, for example, may be separated, and a good Christian counselor may bring the two of them together to negotiate peace and harmony.

Jesus brought peace into the broken relationship between God and man through His own shed blood on the cross (Gal. 3:19–20; Titus 2:14). It's the Lord Jesus Christ who has reconciled believers to God. As the God-man, He is the only person qualified to save the world through His death on the cross and mediate between God and man.

Christ's death is sufficient, and Jesus gave Himself as the "ransom for all" (v 6). A ransom is the price to be paid for the release of a slave or a condemned man. The stated ransom for the release of condemned sinners was the precious shed blood of Christ (1 Peter 1:18–19). Because our debt is paid in full, it no longer exists.

Right now, our nation's debt continues to grow. No one knows how many decades it will take to pay back the trillions of dollars owed. It's hard to imagine ever being debt-free again. Spiritually speaking, the sin debt of mankind is even worse. In fact, it's impossible for any person to pay the debt owed to God because of sin. Man's personal righteousness is like dirty rags in God's eyes (Isa. 64:6). But, because of the cross, we are debt free because Jesus paid it all. Therefore, those in Christ are free from the penalty of sin.

Christ is our substitute. He gave His life "for all" (v 6). The Greek word translated as "for" means "on behalf of."[5] Christ offered himself as a substitute for sinners, dying in our place. God's judgment came on His own Son in our stead. The Bible says, "He made Him who knew no sin to be sin on our behalf that we might become the righteousness of God in Him" (2 Cor. 5:21).

My friend Tim and I served together as summer missionaries in the former Soviet Union in 1991. After Tim graduated from college, he married the girl he loved and together they adopted two children. One day during a family vacation, the children were swimming and somehow went too far into deep water. In desperation, although he was not a good swimmer, Tim tried to swim out to help them. The good news is that he could get both of them close enough to shore to save them. The tragic news is that Tim was so drained from the traumatic rescue that he didn't make it back to shore and drowned. Tim couldn't bear the thought of losing his children, so instead he gave his all to save them even though it cost him his life. Jesus so loved us that He gave his own life that we might live. He came to rescue us from sin even though He had to die a cruel death to accomplish it.

Jesus is the only way to God (John 14:6; Acts 4:12). The basis of man's relationship with God is Christ's redemptive work. We're saved not by our good works but by the grace of God in Christ (Eph 2:8–9). It's the mercy of God through His Son, not our own works, that has enabled us to be regenerated by the Holy Spirit (Titus 3:5).

God's servants are commissioned to proclaim the gospel to all (v 7).

Good news is meant to be spread. God wants everyone to be saved, so everyone needs to hear the gospel. Paul was called by God to be a preacher (v 7a). God saved Paul and commissioned him to proclaim the gospel and to be a teacher to the Gentiles (v 7b). God is still calling His servants to proclaim the good news of salvation through His Son because He is still seeking to save sinners.

We often assume that Americans already know the gospel story. I suppose we think the current generation has heard the gospel just because we heard it. But the gospel only lasts from one generation to the next. We must keep telling the story. If the gospel is not intentionally passed along with clarity, some will miss the good news. All people need to hear and understand.

When Pop icon Dick Clark passed away in 2011, I announced the news of his death to my household. The kids said, "who is Dick Clark?" I thought, "where have you been? Dick Clark was America's oldest teenager; The creator of American Bandstand, and host of the $25,000 Pyramid! How could you not know the name of Dick Clark?" Then I realized that my kids did not grow up watching Dick Clark on television. They really did not know who he was. Many today really do not know the person of Jesus Christ. Do you know why? It is because no one has actually told them about Jesus. They have grown up and somehow missed the most wonderful story ever told. People only come to a saving knowledge of the truth of the gospel if we share it (Rom 10:17).

God's Spirit convicts sinners who hear the gospel to repent and believe (see John 16:5-15).

God is the One who saves. Upon hearing the Gospel of Christ, God the Holy Spirit convicts the hearts of the hearers to repent and place their faith in Christ. He helps people to understand the gospel and their need of salvation. God's people proclaim the gospel to sinners, but God the Holy Spirit is the One who persuades of sin and the need of repentance and faith. Without the help of the Holy Spirit, we would never see the light of the gospel. The Bible teaches that the devil has blinded the minds of lost sinners. Paul says, "But even if our gospel is veiled, it is veiled to those who are perishing, whose minds the god of this age has blinded, who do not believe, lest the light of the gospel of the glory of Christ, who is the image of God, shine on them" (2 Corinthians 4:3-4).

I remember when I was saved. We were having revival services in our church. I do not remember any of the sermon but I remember the time at the end of that church service when I began to understand in my heart that I needed to be saved. My heart seemed so heavy. I knew God was at work in my life. I was only seven years of age but somehow I just knew that it was Jesus knocking on the door of my heart, calling me to let Him come inside (see Rev 3:20). How did I know it was the Lord? Who gave me the understanding as a child? The Holy Spirit did it. He convicts of sin and of the need of salvation (see John 16:7-9). Has the Lord been calling you? Have you trusted in Christ to be your Lord and Savior? This is where the will of God begins for you. If you are uncertain that you are a Christian, you may trust in Him to be your personal Lord and Savior this very moment. Call on Him right now in faith. You may repeat a sinner's prayer like the one below:

> "Dear God, I realize that I am a lost sinner. I understand that Jesus Christ died on the cross and shed His blood to pay for my sins. I believe that He was raised from death on the third day, and He lives. I now repent of my sins and trust in Jesus as my personal Lord and Savior. Lord, I now receive you into my heart by faith. Thank you for saving me. In Jesus name I pray. -Amen"

CHAPTER TWO

SANCTIFICATION: GOD'S WILL IN YOU

"For this is the will of God, your sanctification: that you should abstain from sexual immorality." 1 Thessalonians 4:3

Often, as our sons were coming along, I would ask them an age old question: "What are you going to be when you grow up?" I knew they would become adults and have an impact on others in their particular calling and vocation, but I also knew that they had to mature before they would be ready for the world. Parenting is helping children grow into adulthood in a godly fashion. We want them to do great things after they are grown, but we know that they must mature before they can become the best firemen, business men and women, nurses, teachers, missionaries, and the like. Our Father in heaven knows that spiritually we should mature also. Spiritual maturity through the Lord Jesus Christ is always the will of God for all of His children.

You may be tempted to skip this chapter. Many people asking about God's will simply desire to know what God wants them to "do." This vital chapter is not about "doing." It is about "being." According to the Bible, the will of God is more about being a person who walks in fellowship with God than it is about doing something for Him. God certainly has a special work for every person to do, but Christ-like character matters most. God wants us to be the right kind of people. He wants to do a great work *in* us before He does a great work *through* us. The priority of our Heavenly Father is to shape us into the likeness of His Son (Rom 8:29). This sacred work of the Holy Spirit in the lives of believers is called sanctification. All believers should know what it means and how the process works.

The Meaning of Sanctification

Sanctification is the work of the Holy Spirit in the life of believers to shape them into the likeness of Jesus Christ. "Sanctify" comes from a Greek word meaning "holy" or "set-apart." To be sanctified is to be set apart or made holy by God. This is God's will for every follower of Christ. God wants you to be like His Son. No part of His plan for your life is more important than your own spiritual growth. Whatever God calls you to do for Him will only be fruitful if you are becoming a better person. He wants you to develop into a loving, joyful, patient, godly, and kind member of the Body of Christ. The Holy Spirit of God indwells believers to gently shape us into Christ-likeness.

A three stage process

The Bible reveals the sanctifying work of the Holy Spirit in three inseparable stages. Our salvation has a beginning, a progression, and a conclusion. It all began the moment we were born again. God is faithful to save sinners and work in them until He completes them in Christ at the consummation of the age. Paul was completely confident that God would finish what He started in the lives of Christians: "Being confident of this very thing, that He who has begun a good work in you will complete it until the day of Jesus Christ" (Philippians 1:6).

Justification (Positional Sanctification)

Sanctification begins the moment a person is saved. The Holy Spirit sets apart the believer for Jesus Christ at his conversion (1 Pet 1:2). This doctrine is also known as Justification. A lost person is given a new *position of righteousness* before God in an instant by simply trusting in the work of Christ as payment for their sin. In Christ, a person is cleansed of all their sin and made new: "Therefore, if anyone is in Christ, he is a new creature; old things have passed away; behold, all things have become new (2 Cor 5:17).

Progressive Sanctification

Becoming a new creation in Christ is only the beginning. The process of being shaped into the likeness of Christ is the daily task of the Holy Spirit within every believer. God continually molds us with His hand like the potter molds clay (Jer 18:6). Christians should increase in personal holiness as they walk in the will of God. As we learn and apply the truths of Scripture, our minds are renewed and we mature in our walk with the Lord, and we are able to discern and do His will (Rom 12:2). No follower of Christ reaches spiritual perfection until He takes us home to heaven.

Glorification (Perfect Sanctification)

The sanctifying work of the Holy Spirit will culminate when the saints are taken into the presence of God and redeemed utterly. This is the doctrine of glorification. In the presence of Christ, believers will be complete. Their mortal bodies will be transformed into eternal ones like that of the resurrected body of the Lord Jesus Christ (Rom 8:30; 1 Cor 15:51-53).

The Mandate of Sanctification

Sanctification is the will of God in the life of every true follower of Christ. While Jesus was walking on earth he prayed for all His disciples to be sanctified (see John 17). It is a mandatory work of the Holy Spirit in the life of every believer. Paul wrote, "This is the will of God for you your sanctification" (1 Thess 4:3a). Holiness is not optional: "Be ye holy as I am holy"(1 Peter 1:16). A true believer should not attempt to skip holiness of life to do some work for God. A holy life is the will of God.

One way the believer is to be set apart is in sexual purity (1 Thess 4:3). Adults, college students, and teens who really want to please God and do His will must understand that sexual purity is still essential to our maturity in Christ. Our society has come to scoff at the idea of sexual abstinence before marriage. The world has opted for "safer sex." Pop culture says the church is too restrictive, but believers live by God's standards not social norms. The cross requires us to live counter culturally in many instances. Waiting until marriage and having sexual relations within the confines of the marriage relationship between a man and woman is certainly the will of God (see Matt 19:1-10). The one who refuses to "possess his own vessel in sanctification and honor" (1 Thess 4:4b) will suffer some consequences. Paul warned the church that the Lord is the "avenger" and will hold accountable each person who takes "advantage" or defrauds another through any sexual immorality, "for God did not call us to uncleanness but to holiness" (1 Thess 4:6-7). Anyone who treats God's boundaries for sexual immorality with in-difference will eventually be confronted by its consequences.

One day while I was jogging around the neighborhood, I quickly became aware of the next door neighbor's pit bulldog. He was barking at me as if I was to be his lunch. The neighbor had the beastly canine chained to a tree in the front of his house. I knew he could not possibly break the chain so I did not take the threat seriously. In fact, I even laughed at that vicious dog and treated him with a bit of contempt. I did not think it mattered because he was securely chained and could not possibly touch me. I continued to jog and rounded the circle again to pass by my restrained opponent. As I passed the second time, the dog lunged toward me with all of his might. The chain pulled loose and the pit bull was on my heels within seconds. At this point I was not laughing. The dog leaped u-p and latched on to my right hand. I stopped in my tracks. He held onto me until his master called him off. It was a God thing that the owner was outside. I was delivered!

Sexual immorality is much like that pit bull. You may think you have it chained and under control but it will chase you down and attack you. It will terrorize your marriage relationship world without end. You will have to continually look to the Master to deliver you. It is wise to live within God's boundaries for purity. God does not want sex unleashed before marriage because He knows that outside of that sacred union sexual immorality is a ravenous animal out to destroy intimacy.

Sex in only one area. God calls for holiness in every aspect of life. Whatever God has called you to do for Him should be done with Christ-like character. "Being" always comes before "doing." It is the will of God for all believers to be the right kind of people. What we do will not be very effective if we do not live to please the Lord. God will not be pleased with any good work that has been disconnected from a godly walk. Discussions on God's will often include issues like vocation, education, finding the right person to marry, or a critical decision to be made, but little thought is given to the will of God to walk in righteousness moment by moment of each day. The will of God is first about sanctification or holy living. Serving the Lord and discovering His will overflows from a sanctified walk with God. The young man who wants to marry a godly young lady in the future should discipline himself to be godly now. The best way to find "Mrs. Right" is to be the right Kind of person. The High School student who desires to know which university to attend or what career to pursue should already be working on becoming a person of integrity. Character is essential to every endeavor. Whatever a person decides to do with his life will only have a profound impact for God's kingdom if that person is being Christ-like as they do it. No believer should attempt to do great things for God without serious consideration of their personal holiness. The crux of the matter in the will of God is to follow Jesus and live obediently by faith.

Time to Restart?

It may be time to start over with a fresh pursuit of the will of God. Computers that get infected run slowly. If the problem is severe enough the computer may shut down completely. We need to be sure that some virus has not infected our spiritual systems. Like a computer, we cannot operate properly until we have been cleaned up and maybe even reprogrammed. The Bible says that God is willing to renew us day by day: "Therefore we do not lose heart. Even though our outward man is perishing, yet the inward man is being renewed day by day" (2 Corinthians 4:16).

Our renewal begins with *Conviction of Sin*. People will never deal with sin that they do not acknowledge. Under the preaching of the truth of the Word of God, the Holy Spirit convicts the hearts of people of sin. A touch of guilt will come into the soul of a child of God who has sinned against Him. It is a good thing. Without conviction of sin we would never feel a need to turn away from it. We may be tempted to think that sin goes unnoticed. People may not know of our secret sins, but God knows all things. The Holy Spirit will bring to our minds anything that is not pleasing to God. He will plead with us to deal with it before the consequences of sin ruin our lives.

Conviction of sin should lead to *Confession and Repentance of Sin*. It is never enough to simply admit sin. The true child of God will confess sin and repent. God is faithful to forgive and cleanse His children from all sin. John says, "If we confess our sin He is faithful and just to forgive our sin and cleanse us from all unrighteousness" (1 John 1:9) *What happened to Already Come?*

The renewal process will be incomplete without a *New Commitment to Walk with the Lord daily*. The heart of every believer ought to obey the Lord's Word and walk in His will moment by moment each day. With a fresh commitment to be in fellowship with the Lord, a believer can take action to do whatever it takes to become more like the Lord Jesus Christ.

The Means of Sanctification

The Holy Spirit of God works in Believers to cause their spiritual growth and maturity. He makes it happen. Paul prayed that the "God of peace" would act in the lives of saints so that they would mature completely in the Faith (1 Thess 5:23). Paul prayed for God to sanctify the saints "completely" (23a). The word translated "completely" is a compound that implies a thing will be done totally and finished completely.[6] God works in the saints that their "whole spirit, soul, and body be preserved blameless at the coming of our Lord Jesus Christ" (v.23b). The Father works willingly in the lives of His children until the finish at the consummation of the age. Believers will receive glorified bodies in the presence of the Lord (Rom 8:30; 1 Cor 15).

God not only calls us, but He is faithful to finish what He starts (1 Thess 5:25). The outcome of our salvation is in the hands of God who is Faithful to complete what He began the moment we trusted in Christ. But God's willingness to sanctify ought to be matched by the willingness of saints to be transformed from the inside out. God wants us to cooperate with His Spirit who is actively shaping us into the image of His Son.

How Believers cooperate in the process

Knowing that sanctification is the will of God for believers should motivate them to cooperate in the process. What can believers do to grow in personal holiness? How does it happen? Christians are responsible to cooperate with the Holy Spirit as He works within to transform lives into Christlikeness. Paul says, "Therefore, my beloved, as you have always obeyed, not as in my presence only, but now much more in my absence, *work out your own salvation* with fear and trembling: For it is God who works in you both to will and to do for His good pleasure" (Philippians 2:12-13).

To "work out" salvation is not about working to be saved or justified before God. We are forgiven of all of our sins the moment we trust in Christ to be Lord and Savior. Paul was not telling the church to work in order to be saved, but exhorting them to labor in their efforts to mature spiritually. God was at work in them already. They needed to cooperate with the indwelling Holy Spirit who was actively shaping them into Christlikeness. They would not develop properly if they neglected to make their best effort in cooperation with the Spirit.

Many people work out daily to stay in shape physically. God has given us a body, but how we treat it will largely determine our health and strength. If we diet properly and exercise we will be much healthier. We can also improve strength by working to build muscle. It takes proper intake and exercise. Spiritual growth works much the same way. God gives spiritual life and causes development, but we have responsibilities as followers of Christ to work toward maturity. The saints need a daily spiritual "workout." So what can believers do to enhance their own spiritual growth? From the Bible we can put together an excellent program for a daily spiritual workout. Consider these eight steps to maturity:

1. Saturate your mind with the truth of the Scripture and apply it.

The truth of the Word of God is essential to spiritual growth. Jesus prayed for the Father to "sanctify them by Your truth. Your word is truth" (Jn 17:17). The Bible is God's written truth given to all mankind: "All Scripture is given by inspiration of God, and is profitable for doctrine, for reproof, for correction, for instruction in righteousness" (2 Tim 3:16). The psalmist asked, "How can a man keep his way pure?" The answer is the Word: "Your word I have hidden in my heart, That I might not sin against you"(Ps 119:11). The spiritual disciplines of reading, meditating, studying, memorizing, and listening to Bible teaching and preaching are essential to the spiritual maturity of believers. The Bible says, "Long for the sincere milk of the word that you may grow in respect to salvation"(1 Peter 2:2). The will of God is intimately connected to the Word of God. The will of God is often discovered much faster when the truth of Scripture permeates and dominates the mind.

I watched a special documentary not long ago of a young person who loved carrots. She had carrots for breakfast, lunch and dinner. She loved carrot juice, carrot tea, carrot casserole or just plain carrots! In fact, she said that she ate so many carrots as a teenager that she began to notice her skin was turning orange. She nearly became a carrot. She was being transformed by what she was taking into her system. If we will continue to take in truth in our hearts and minds, we will begin to live out what is on the inside (Rom 12:2). The truth comes shining through!

What daily effort are you making to take in the truth? Do you read the Bible daily? Do you pray over the Word and listen for the Lord to speak to you? Are you in Sunday School or part of some small group listening to Bible teaching and learning its principles? All the searching you do on-line and surfing the web, how much Scripture and Christ preaching do you log on to? Nothing but the truth will renew the mind. Jesus said, "You shall know the truth and the truth shall set you free" (John 8:32). Knowing and applying the truth will renew the mind and enable the children of God to discern His will (Rom 12:2). Intake should lead to application. The book of James tells us to be sure to apply the truth that we are hearing: "Therefore lay aside all filthiness and overflow of wickedness, and receive with meekness the implanted word, which is able to save your souls. But be doers of the word, and not hearers only, deceiving yourselves" (James 1:21-22).

2. Rely on the Holy Spirit to empower you to obey the truth and serve.

Since the Spirit is responsible to transform, we should learn to depend on Him. The Holy Spirit is God. He indwells every believer to empower them to obey and to shape them into Christlikeness. We must learn to depend on the Holy Spirit to work in us and through us to the glory of God. Growth takes place in an environment of submission. Each obedient application of the truth is used by the Spirit to make us more like Christ. To obey is to progress. To disobey is to suffer a setback. Many people workout with their personal trainer. The trainer guides the workout. He or she provides instruction, encouragement, and accountability. The Spirit is our indwelling personal trainer in spirituality. He works within while we workout. The trainer just wants cooperation and obedience. Progress is made with every act or exercise of submission.

When believers are disobedient the Spirit is "quenched" (1Thess 5:19) and "grieved" (Eph 4:30) which stunts the growth process. The Holy Spirit works freely through a surrendered life. The Bible tells us to "be filled" with the "Spirit" (Eph 5:18), or to "walk in the Spirit" (Gal 5:16) who reproduce the "fruit of the Spirit" (Gal 5:22-23). The Holy Spirit will unleash the power of God in our lives if we will depend on Him as we do His will (Phil 4:13).

Begin serving in some way and you will sense God at work through you. I know you are still on a quest to discover God's will, but do not wait any longer to begin serving and helping others. God wants you to get started now. Get involved in a ministry project in you Sunday School class or youth group. Volunteer to help in a soup kitchen. Be a greeter at church. Go to the care center and spend some time with some of the residents. Whatever you do, let the Holy Spirit empower you to do it to the glory of God. As you serve others in the power of the Holy Spirit, God will increase your faith and make you more like Jesus.

3. Pray for yourself and others to be shaped into the likeness of Christ.

Paul prayed that the local church would grow and become complete in Christ (1 Thess 5:23). Epaphras, a member of the church at Colosse, labored in his prayers for the saints that they would "stand perfect and complete in all the will of God"(Col 4:12). Jesus also prayed for the sanctification of His current followers and the ones to come (see John 17). We should keep asking Him to do His life changing work. God uses the faithful intercessions of His children. We should pray for our own spiritual maturity and pray for other saints to grow as well. I often pray Philippians 1:8-11 or Colossians 1:9-15 for myself, my family and others. Much of our spiritual growth is correlated to the steadfast intercessions of others made on our behalf each day. If you want to make a difference in a person's life, pray for them.

One dear lady had a ministry of intercession. She often told me how she prayed for me as a young ministerial student. I was encouraged to endure the early hardships and to keep pursuing the will of God because I knew people like her prayed for me to grow as a young preacher. Others are encouraged to keep the Faith and persevere in their pursuit of the will of God when they know that saints are making intercession for them. Missionaries, evangelists, pastors, and other servants of God who may be enduring persecution and tribulation can stay faithful to the Lord due to the fact that some saint prays for them. New Christians will be protected from the adversary who will tempt them to mess up and give up on their journey with the Lord. The devil will use adversity to attempt to trip them up. God allows trials to enhance their spiritual growth. Praying people can make a difference.

4. Build relationships with godly Christians.

Having right relationships is a critical element in our journey toward godliness. This is why being involved in a church, specifically a small group within a church, is so important. We need other believers to help us become the persons God designed for us to be. Others can build us up or tear us down. Keeping company with the wrong kind of people will often lead to compromise. The Bible says, "Do not be deceived: Evil company corrupts good habits" (1 Cor 15:33). We need relationships that stimulate and challenge us to become like Christ. The local church is a body of believers who are responsible for mutual edification. The Author of Hebrews says, "And let us consider one another in order to stir up love and good works, not forsaking the assembling of ourselves together, as is the manner of some, but exhorting one another, and so much more as you see the day approaching" (Hebrews 10:24-25). We need one another. It is dangerous for believers to be inconsistent in attending church. We all need Spiritually mature friends who will encourage us and hold us accountable in our walk with the Lord. The Bible says, "Iron sharpens iron so a man sharpens the countenance of his friend" (Proverbs 27:17).

Some Christians wisely choose a friend, usually the same gender, for mutual accountability meetings and prayer on a regular basis. They share their weaknesses, confess their sins, offer advice, and pray for one another to walk faithfully with the Lord. All things are confidential. Ask the Lord to show you a person who will be a trustworthy accountability partner to help you grow spiritually.

5. Persevere through trials knowing that we are maturing in the faith.

This one is difficult to accept and apply. The Bible teaches us to count it joy when we are tried and tested because we know that God is at work to build your character (James 1:2-4). You may be enduring some trial as you are reading. You may be seeking the Lord's will as to what you should do in the midst of such tribulation. It is comforting to know that almighty God is in control of all things and that He only allows what will accomplish good in the lives of His own (Rom 8:28-29). The children of God need not be fearful in any circumstance (Isa 41:10).

God even uses chastisement to train us in righteous (see Heb 12:3-11). God never leads us to sin (James 1:13), but He disciplines His children who rebel against Him. Loving parents correct their children because they desire the best for them. Our Loving heavenly Father also chastises us when we are disobedient because He wants us to have a better life of righteous living. Chastening is good. It is proof we are indeed the children of God (Heb 12:7-8). We must receive this truth by faith, or we may grow weary before God accomplishes His purpose. The writer of Hebrews reminds us that God's loving discipline will pay off in the end: "Now no chastening seems to be joyful for the present, but painful; nevertheless, afterward it yields the peaceable fruit of righteousness to those who have been trained by it" (Hebrews 12:11). God is at work to give us Christ-like character through the trials and even the chastisement we may be enduring. Persevere. Do not quit. God is working all things together for good to conform us to the image of Christ (see Rom 8:28-29). How can true disciples endure testing and remain faithful till the end? Jesus will help. The entire sanctification process is God's work. We must always look to the Lord.

6. Focus on the Lord Jesus Christ at all times.

Jesus is *"the author and finisher of our faith" (Heb 12:2)*. The writer of Hebrews insisted that believers keep looking to Jesus lest they be tempted to turn away from their faith in Christ and fall back into their old way of religion. Christian discipleship is not merely religion but a personal relationship with the Son of God. The word "looking" speaks of looking away from everything else and focusing on a person or object that captures the heart.[7] We should have eyes for Jesus only.

When a bride come down the aisle on her wedding day, she focuses on her husband to be. She looks to him alone. He is the one who has captured her heart with unconditional love. He is the person that she will be joined with for life. The bride has faith in him that he will be true to his word and never leave her nor forsake her.

True disciples of the Lord Jesus must keep their eyes on Jesus to mature in the Faith. Why? The writer of Hebrews gives three good reasons for growing disciples to fix their eyes on Jesus. We should fix our eyes on Jesus because of who He is, what He has done, and where He is seated.

First, we should fix our eyes on Jesus because of *who* He is: "the author and finisher of our faith" (v.2). As "Author," Jesus is the "originator," "founder," and "champion" of the Christian faith.[8] He is the perfect example of obedience in the will of God. Of all the great examples of men and women who lived by faith listed in Hebrews 11, there is none just like Jesus. He made them faithful. They all kept their focus on Him. We may glance at the faithful but we fixate on the Lord Jesus. He is the "Author and finisher" of our Christian walk! He started a great work in us and he will complete it (Phil 1:6).

Second, we should fix our eyes upon Jesus because of *what* He has done: Jesus "endured the cross (v.2b)." Jesus died on the cross to atone for our sin that we could be saved and transformed into His likeness. What shame and suffering He endured in the will of God. We will suffer persecution, tribulation, and trial but nothing like our Lord did. All pain and suffering in the will of God pales in comparison to the passion of Christ. He persevered until the end. And in His name so can you. We should keep our eyes on Jesus as we run the race to the finish (Heb 12:1).

Third, we should keep our eyes on Jesus because of *where* He is seated: "at the right hand of God" (v.2c). There He is seated in the highest place watching over us and interceding for us as we run the race. He is seated in the place of sovereign power. He rules and reigns from on High. Unlike those other faithful followers who have passed on, Jesus lives to give strength and wisdom to those who look to Him. The things of this world that may distract us from our devotion to God. We must chose to keep our eyes on Jesus who will lead us to a faithful finish. Can you see Him in glory?

7. Anticipate the imminent return of Jesus Christ

Paul prayed for the saints to be "preserved blameless at the second coming of Christ" (1 Thess 5:23c). The prayer is one of expectancy. Looking forward to that blessed day when Jesus Christ comes back again will motivate believers to remain true to Him until the end of the age. No man can know the hour or the day (Matt 24:36). It could be today. Are you ready for Jesus Christ to come back to earth again?

8. Die to self

Sanctification will not progress until the believer practices dying to self. Like a seed planted in fertile soil, one has to die in order to live spiritually and bear fruit (John 12:24). To follow Christ is to give up personal preferences and take up a cross each day (Luke 9:23-24). Bearing a cross means to suffer the loss of some things and some relationships in order to follow Christ in His will; love for God must take precedence (Matt 10:34-42). Paul counted everything as "rubbish" to become more like Jesus (Phil 3:8).

The disciple's death to self is depicted in baptism because we "died to sin" and have been made "alive to God" (Rom 6:2-4). A Christian dies to the old way of life at conversion and continues to crucify the flesh daily and lives by faith (Gal 2:20). If a Christian refuses to die to himself, all of these other disciplines like Bible intake, worship, prayer, meditation, giving, serving, fellowship and the like will be useless to spiritual growth. True disciples must offer themselves as "living sacrifices" before God if they desire to mature in the Faith and do His will (Rom 12:1-2). The spiritual obituary of the believer who has died to self should include leaving behind *selfish appetites*, *selfish ambitions*, and *self-adequacy*.

We must die to our selfish appetites. Man is born with many natural and fleshly desires, but he must keep them in check, else they will take control of him. Ever since the Garden of Eden, the old serpent has used man's appetite to tempt him to rebel and have his needs met outside of God's will.

Our natural appetites are given by God. They are not evil. God knows that mankind has many needs like food, water, rest, love, friendship, companionship, sex, acceptance, and recognition. Only when man seeks to meet these needs in a way that is displeasing to God has he become perverted. The need for food and water, without self-discipline, becomes self-indulgence and gluttony. The need for rest, which is good, can slide into slothfulness and laziness. Lust can become a cheap imitation for genuine love. Friendship can deteriorate into merely using people as a means of personal gain. Companionship or sexual intimacy, which is a gift from God to be shared between a husband and his wife in a lifelong commitment, often becomes a temporal arrangement because one or the other finds someone else to meet their physical and emotional "needs." The desire for acceptance and recognition, left unchecked, can drive a person to do all kinds of foolish things if they do not understand how completely they are accepted in Christ Jesus (Eph 1:6). Believers are not to be controlled by their passions but "filled with the Spirit" and under His influence (Eph 5:18).

Upon trusting Christ, the believer, in that moment, "crucified the flesh along with its passions and desires"(Gal 5:24). Yet, the flesh constantly cries out to be satisfied so believers must "walk in the Spirit" and refuse to indulge in these fleshly desires (Gal 5:16).

Christians must exercise self-control in the strength of the Lord. Paul said, "But I discipline my body and bring it into subjection, lest, when I have preached to others, I myself should be disqualified" (2 Cor 9:27).

We must die to our selfish ambition. The will of God is not about me. It's all about Jesus. Our only true ambition should be to follow Him and do a work that brings Him honor and glory (Gal 6:14). Since the Fall, man has a natural inclination to exalt himself and do his own thing. Paul lists "selfish ambitions" among the many vices of the wicked who have no part in God's kingdom (Gal 5:20). The word was used of those seeking political position and power for the purpose of self-promotion.[9] "Selfish ambitions" may seem harmless, but they too are wicked works of the flesh along with "adultery, fornication, uncleanness, lewdness, idolatry, sorcery, hatred, contentions, jealousies, outbursts of wrath, ...dissensions, heresies, envy, murders, drunkenness, revelries, and the like..." (vv.20-21). The heart of believers, even those in positions of leadership, should be to serve others, not to rule over them. Jesus did not come to be served but to serve and gave His life for sinners (Matt 20:28; Mark 10:45).

We must die to our self-adequacy. The deeds of the flesh can only be overcome by the power of the Holy Spirit (Gal 5:16). Believers must die to the notion that the will of God can be done in their own personal strength. Human nature seeks to live a good life and to accomplish many good works through self-will, knowledge, experience, and talent. But no one is good but God and no good can be done without Him (Matt 19:17). Paul understood that "our sufficiency is from God"(2 Cor 3:5). Without abiding in Christ, men and their ministries will be fruitless (John 15:4). Christlike character, or the "fruit of the Spirit," is reproduced in the lives of believers as they "walk by the Spirit" and depend on His power (Gal 5:16; 22-23). Christians must be careful to depend on the power of Christ to do the will of God (Phil 4:13).

We dare not place our hope in anything in this old world but Christ alone. Dietrich Bonhoeffer was right to say, "When Christ calls a man, he bids him come and die."[10]

The following essay spoke to my heart so poignantly and personally. Ironically, it was written anonymously. I suppose the author simply chose to die to self, receiving no accolades or praise for these touching and insightful words:

When you are forgotten, or neglected, or purposefully set at naught,
And you don't sting and hurt with the insult or the oversight, but
your heart is happy being counted worthy to suffer for Christ,
That is dying to self.

When your good is evil spoken of,
When your wishes are crossed, your advice disregarded, your opinions ridiculed,
And you refuse to let anger rise in your heart, or even defend yourself, but take it all in patient loving silence,
That is dying to self.

When you lovingly and patiently bear any disorder, any irregularity, and impunctuality, or any annoyance,
When you can stand face to face with waste, folly, extravagance, spiritual insensibility,
And endure it as Jesus endured it,
That is dying to self.

When you are content with any food, any offering, any raiment, any climate,
any society, any solitude, any interruption
By the will of God,
That is dying to self.

*When you never care to refer to yourself in conversation, or record your own
good works, or itch after commendation,*
When you can truly love to be unknown,
That is dying to self.

*When you can see your brother prosper and have his needs met, and
can honestly*
rejoice with him in spirit and feel no envy nor question God,
While your own needs are far greater and in desperate circumstances,
That is dying to self.

*When you can receive correction and reproof from one of less stature
than yourself,*
and can humbly submit inwardly as well as outwardly,
finding no rebellion or resentment rising within your heart,
That is dying to self.

-Anonymous

Check list for Spiritual Growth

It may be helpful to spend some quiet time evaluating your personal
involvement in these disciplines. Review the following eight
principles for growth to see if you are making your best effort to
grow in your walk with the Lord Jesus Christ.

1) We should saturate our minds with the truth of Scripture and
   apply it.
2) We should rely on the Holy Spirit to empower us to obey and
   serve.
3) We should pray for ourselves and others to be made like Christ.
4) We should build relationships with godly Christians.
5) We should persevere through trials which mature us.
6) We should focus on the Lord Jesus Christ at all times

7) We should anticipate the imminent return of Jesus Christ.
8) We should die to self.

A crucial question

Before moving forward with our pursuit of the will of God, we need to be sure that our personal commitment to the Lordship of Jesus Christ in unwavering. Are you determined to "be" the person God desires for you to be without knowing the details of His will for your life? Are you willing to continue to take in the truth, pray, and persevere in the power of the Holy Spirit until God shows you the next step?

CHAPTER THREE

SOMETHING SPECIAL: GOD'S WILL THROUGH YOU

*"For we are His workmanship, created in Christ Jesus
for good works, which God prepared beforehand that
we should walk in them." Ephesians 2:10*

God has a personal plan for your life. Something special. It's as unique as your own finger print. God made only one of you, and He has preordained a special work that only you can complete for His glory (Eph 2:10). He has graced you with wisdom, talent, and at least one gift from His Holy Spirit to serve others in His power and bring glory to Himself (1 Peter 4:10-11).

The most troubling issue with God's personal will is that often we just cannot figure out exactly what it is that God desires for us to do. We know that we should certainly live by the principles of the Bible, but how can we know the part of God's will that is not spelled out for us in His Word? The problem reminds me of the popular G.I. Joe action figure that I owned as a kid. Modern readers will find it hard to believe, but our toys in the seventies were not often electronic. My G.I. Joe had no batteries or any other power source. He only had a pull string coming right out of his back. I thought he was one cool conqueror. When I pulled the string G.I. Joe would firmly give the command for the mission: "I have a tough assignment for you." The only problem I had with G.I. Joe is that he never said anything else. I knew that he had a "tough assignment" for me, but I did not have a clue about what I was supposed to do. I am sure this is the way many sincere followers of Christ often feel. Many Christians are ready to take on a "tough assignment" for the Kingdom of God. They want to do the will of God, but they just do not know what God wants them to do. They love Jesus. They have faith. They are ready to go to the ends of the earth if God would just help them to see clearly what He wants them to do. If this is the way you have been feeling, keep reading. Keep praying. Keep believing. Do not give up. You are not the first to struggle with knowing God's will. All of us at one time or another have wondered what to do next. In time, the pathway God has designed for your walk of life will become clear.

Fishin' in the fog

One of my favorite things to do as a lad was go fishin'. Every summer our family and some of our closest friends would take a vacation in the North Georgia Mountains in a little town called Hiawassee. (What do you mean you have never heard of it?) We stayed weeks at a time in these little cabins along side of Lake Chatuge. I remember wishing the school year would end so I could grab my tackle and run off to the mountains.

One morning just before daybreak, four of us quietly walked down to the dock, climbed in our little boat, and eased away from the camp. I just knew we would match the catch of Jesus disciples and fill the boat to overflowing with fish that morning. We were moving along and enjoying the ride until suddenly we ran through a white wall- a wall of fog. Have you ever been in a mountain fog? It was like the clouds of heaven had just swallowed us up. We could hardly see one another. The driver slowed the boat to a drift and then finally stopped near the shore and dropped anchor. We were going nowhere. This was unexpected. I was so disappointed. Perhaps, even a little angry. I was out there to catch the "big one," but now all I could do was sit and wait.

Your pursuit of God's will may be like the genesis of our fishing trip. You want to get on with the exciting journey, but you find yourself sitting in the fog. It seems like you are wasting time. You may be feeling frustrated, even tempted to give up on the will of God completely. The Christian life is supposed to be a great adventure, but it seems life is going nowhere. Waiting in a spiritual fog does not mean that you have strayed. God often requires His children to wait. The Lord uses delays as a tool of teaching. Meditate on these verses that call on the people of God to wait on the Lord:

> "Wait on the Lord; Be of good courage, and He shall strengthen you heart; Wait, I say, on the Lord!
> -Psalm 27:14

> "Wait on the Lord. And keep His way. And He shall exalt you to inherit the land; when the wicked are cut off, you shall see it"
> -Psalm 37:34

> "But those who wait on the Lord shall renew their strength; They shall mount up with wings like eagles, they will run and not be weary, they shall walk and not faint."
>
> -Isaiah 40:31

Back in the boat

There we were in our little fishing boat afloat in a heavy fog. After about five minutes of sitting speechless, the oldest fellow aboard made a move. Without saying a word, he reached over and picked up his rod and reel. He baited his hook and cast his line as far out into that fog as he could. None of us saw where the line went. We only heard it hit the water with a gentle splash. He then turned to the rest of us and said, "Ya'll know what? It's just as well that we fish. Who knows? We might catch one right here as good as anywhere on this lake." I thought that was the perfect response to a bad situation. I never forgot what he said. God taught me something that morning. When you do not know what to do next just fish right where you are. Just keep working as you wait on God to show you the next step in His plan for your life. The fog will go away in His time.

After about an hour of sitting still and fishing, the fog finally lifted. The sun broke through so radiantly that the fog disappeared almost as fast as it had engulfed us earlier that morning. We could plainly see where we were going. And go we did. We moved quickly down the lake to one of our favorite coves and caught a basket full of bream. I was one happy boy!

The same is going to be true with your journey in the will of God if you are willing to wait on the Lord. The right thing for you do is "fish" right where you are until God shows you what to do next. You may feel as if you are in a thick fog without a clue of what direction to go. If God has not yet shown you what He desires for you, then He has a reason for the delay. Trust Him. Keep doing what you know God has called you to do until He shows you the next step of His divine plan. In His time, the fog will lift and you will finally see the light.

How to discern the will of God

If you are in the fog when it comes to discovering the will of God, you are not alone. We all struggle at times to know what to do. I am certain that I have missed God's best for my life on occasion. I am thankful that God is merciful and helps us to pick up the pieces and start again. Even if you have made some major mistakes in your life, it is not too late to make a change for the better. God is still willing to give wisdom and direction to any of His children who call on Him in faith (James 1:5-8).

I have learned that the way to discern the next step in God's plan for me is to obey the principles that are taught in the Bible. This is the basic premise of this book. Daily obedience to the truth will prepare our hearts and minds to discern and do God's will. Discipleship leads to discovery. No one will miss the will of God if they are walking with Jesus each day. Follow the Lord and He will show you what He wants you to be and do. The truth of the Word will transform the mind of faithful followers to understand what pleases God. Paul called this process the renewal of the mind: "And do not be conformed to this world, but be transformed by the renewal of your mind that you may prove what is that good and acceptable and perfect will of God"
(Romans 12:2).

Four Basic Steps

Applying four fundamental principles from the Word of God will lead us to God's personal will for our lives. I have learned that following the known will of God that has been written for us in the Bible is essential to finding the unknown path that God would have us to follow. When we obey what we know to be true, God will begin to show us His plan for our lives one step at a time. Why would God reveal more to us if we are uninterested in obeying what is already spelled out in His Word? The Psalmist understood the principle: "Thy Word is a lamp unto my feet; and a light unto my path" (Psalm 119:105). The Word of God illuminates the path for His children to know how to walk in His will. Reading and meditating upon Scripture trains the mind and human spirit to hear the voice of the Lord. A prompting of the Holy Spirit will impress our hearts and show us the direction we should go. A verse that God has used on many occasions to direct me in His will is First Thessalonians 5:18. The "will of God" is specifically given for all believers to obey: "In everything give thanks, for this is the will of God in Christ Jesus for you" (1 Thess 5:18).

It is God's will that all of His children continually come to Him and give thanks. After memorizing this verse, I began to study the entire passage of Scripture in its context. I became aware of four wonderful principles that helped me to discover the next step in God's personal will for my life. Take time to read the passage:

"Rejoice always,
pray without ceasing,
in everything give thanks; for this is the will of God in
Christ Jesus for you.
Do not quench the Spirit.
Do not despise prophecies.
Test all things; hold fast what is good.
Abstain from every form of evil.
Now may the God of peace Himself sanctify you completely;
and may your whole spirit, soul, and body be preserved blameless
at the coming of our Lord Jesus Christ.
He who calls you is faithful, who will also do it."

- 1 Thess 5:16-24

As I absorbed this passage into my mind, I could sense the Lord at work in my life. He would show me the next step in His will as I began to apply the truth of His Word in my life each day. Living by the principles of the Word of God will place believers on a path to discovering the divine purpose and plan for their lives. It is the greatest of adventures. God will not reveal it all at once but gives perfect light to take the next step along the way. Letting the Word of the Lord guide our steps will take us places we never thought we would be able to go and involve us in lives of people whom we will never forget. It all begins with simple obedience. From God's Word, I learned four fundamental phases of discovery:

(1) Pray for the will of God (1 Thess 5:17-18).
(2) Perceive the will of God (1 Thess 5:19-20).
(3) Prove (test) the will of God (1 Thess 5:21a).
(4) Possess the will of God (1 Thess 5:21b).

Continuing to follow these four basic principles that Paul passed along to the Thessalonians has given me a blessed assurance that I am discerning God's will clearly. How can I go wrong obeying God's Word? I have become much more confident in moving forward by faith when I know that I have closely followed the principles of Scripture. I honestly believe this is one way the Holy Spirit keeps believers on the right path. Believers who daily walk in the power of the Holy Spirit to obey the truth can be confident that they will be given discernment, wisdom, insight, and knowledge about their future. If we will obey what we know to be true of God's will for lives, in His time, He will show us the next step. The journey begins by spending time in prayer and fellowship with our heavenly Father through meditating on His Word. This God-given privilege and responsibility of ongoing prayer is what we will give ourselves to in the next chapter.

CHAPTER FOUR

PRAYING FOR GOD'S WILL

"Pray without ceasing"1 Thessalonians 5:17

O ur second son, Aaron, was on the drum line in his high school marching band. He understands the importance of keeping the rhythm because the entire band marches, at least in part, to the beat of the drummers. If we are to keep in step with God, prayer must be constant in our walk with the Lord, much like the beat of the drummers to a marching band. Abiding prayer is a key component of discovering the will of God. Daily prayer and meditation in God's Word positions believers to hear from the Lord, and keeps them in rhythm with the Holy Spirit's agenda. An intimate relationship with Christ is crucial to hearing from God and understanding His will.

Jesus habitually prayed alone in fellowship with God the Father early in the morning (Mark 1:35). He also prayed to the Father in the garden of Gethsemane to affirm the Father's will before His crucifixion (Matt 26:30-36). If Jesus made prayer a priority and repeatedly called on the Father concerning His will, should we not do the same? Persistent prayer is essential to knowing God and His will for our lives.

The Bible commands believers to "pray without ceasing" and to "give thanks" in every circumstance (1 Thess 5:17-18). It is always the will of God for His children to pray and give thanks. The two are intrinsical. We should be thankful as we pray knowing that God is in control and providing all of our needs. We should be thankful before God because we know that He will show us what He desires for us to do and give us the grace to accomplish great things for His glory. Praying with a grateful heart draws us closer to God and prepares our hearts to hear from Him. In prayer, believers should be *submissive, Scriptural, specific, steadfast,* and *sensitive* to the leadership of the Holy Spirit to stay in touch with God and understand His will each day.

Be Submissive

We must be submissive in prayer for God's will. The best way to begin praying about the will of God is to commit ourselves to do His will before He reveals it. In First Thessalonians 5:17, The word Paul uses for "pray" is a general word for prayer that refers to approaching God with worship in mind.[11] We should come with pure hearts and an attitude of submission. Our desire should be to please Him. The Christian life is about worshiping, honoring, and bringing glory to God. The will of God is about His purpose and plan for His people. We want to discover His will and gladly follow.

Concerning the will of the Father, Jesus, God's own Son, prayed with a submissive heart: "Not my will but thine be done" (Matt 26:36,42). We too should pray for God's will in our lives with the same attitude of submission and obedience (Phil 2:5-11). Jesus was willing to do the will of the Father at any cost. He also taught His disciples to pray for God's kingdom rule to come and God's will to be done (Matt 6:10). Prayer is one way God aligns believers with His will and kingdom agenda. We connect and relate to God personally in prayer. Fellowship with the Lord through prayer is essential to a growing relationship with Him. A submissive attitude in prayer honors God our Father for who He is. Any young man speaking with his father should respect him. He is the father. Any believer should approach God the Father with humility and reverence because He is Holy God. He knows all things. He knows what is best for us.

God may call you to the mission field. Are you willing to go? God may lead you into an area of ministry that takes you out of your comfort zone. Are you willing to do it? The Holy Spirit may be prompting you to attend a different college or university than you planned. Are you willing to adjust? The Lord's will for you may be something that has never crossed your mind. Are you willing to submit to God's plan for your life without knowing all of the details? We should pray like the prophet Isaiah who volunteered to serve the Lord *before* he knew what God was calling him to do, saying, "Here am I, send me" (6:8).

Be Scriptural

The Bible is the written Word of God. Learning to pray according to the principles taught in Scripture will prepare our hearts and minds to hear from God. Jesus taught His disciples to pray by giving them a model prayer (Matt 6: 5-15; Luke 11:2-4).

Applying the model prayer of Jesus daily is central to walking with God and discovering His will. Elizabeth Elliott concurs: "A thoughtful consideration of the words of the Lord's prayer will help us to put our minds in the right frame before we begin knocking on God's door for guidance in some particular matter. This is the model prayer Jesus gave His disciples when they asked him to teach them to pray. It is all-inclusive and therefore furnishes the context for all prayers, including, "Lead me, Lord. Show me what to do."[12]

If prayer, according the teachings of Jesus, is part of daily devotion, the will of God will be often be discovered and understood much easier. Daily prayer and discipleship will lead to discovery.

Two of the petitions of Jesus directly applied to God's kingdom and God's will on earth (Matt 6:10). Believers who follow the teachings of Jesus pray for God's will to be done in their lives each day.

Be Specific

The model prayer of Jesus is intended to be an outline for praying. The Lord did not mean for His disciples to merely quote the Scripture as a prayer but to add their personal and specific needs. We should also be specific in our praying for God's will. Ask God about the particular thing you need to know. Many have learned to pray generally but not very specifically. General praying may mean that we are not taking the command to pray seriously. God wants His children to share every desire and concern with Him. He cares about every desire of the heart. Therefore, we should be specific in prayer about the things we want God to do for us.

On my fourteenth birthday, I wanted a new rod and reel. I told my father exactly what I wanted. I even made the trip to the sports section of the Roses department store to pick it out myself. I gave Dad all the needed information. I told him the name brand, the price, the length, and the color. I think I even left it on the end of the rack so it would be easy for him to find. Guess what I received? Right. The very thing for which I asked. Pop always gave us what we asked for unless he knew that the things we desired were not best for us.

God is a loving Father who will give His children the very best. He does not need to be informed about what we need because He already knows. God knows all things. He knows what we need before we ever ask. Why then should we be so specific in prayer? I think one good reason is so that we will know just how well God listens to His children and desires to hear from us and meet our needs and desires. Answered prayer is an expression of His unconditional love. God provides for His children. He does not deceive or give less than we need. Jesus taught the disciples to ask specifically and assured them that God would give them their asked requests. Jesus said, "Or what man is there among you who, if his son asked for bread, will give him a stone? Or if he asked for a fish, will he give him aserpent? If you them, being evil, know how to give good gifts to your children, how much more will your Father in heaven give good things to those who ask Him" (Matthew 7:9-11). Jesus also promised, "Therefore I say to you, whatever things you ask when you pray, believe that you receive them, and you will have them" (Mark 11:24).

God the Father often gives His children exactly what they asked for. Why not ask specifically? God will show us His will if we will ask. No matter the need in your life or the desire of your heart, you can come to God with your specific petition and believe that God is going to answer your prayer. Does God always answer prayer? Yes. He may not always give us the answer we want, but He always answers the prayers of His children. He will sometimes answer "yes, this is my will for you." He will sometimes answer "no, this is not my will." He will sometimes answer "wait." All three are answers. We simply have to trust God our Father to know what is best for His children and trust Him to answer according to His will (Proverbs 3:5-6). Trusting God means waiting on Him to do His will in His time. The Bible promises answers to those who pray, trust, and wait. God promises to take care of His own. God said to Jeremiah, "I know the plans that I have for you says the Lord. Plans for welfare and not for calamity, to give you a future and a hope" (Jeremiah 29:11-13). And God promised to answer prayer and reveal His will: "Call to Me and I will answer you I will tell you great and mighty things that you do not know" (Jeremiah 33:3).

God will certainly keep His promises. If you are praying and believing God to show you His will, rest assured, He will show you. I know it is hard to wait in the fog. You may be frustrated because you have been praying for weeks and still do not know what to do. Just keep praying. There is a good reason for the delay. God is working in your life to make you more like Christ. The need to know His will for your life has driven you to your knees in prayer. You are seeking God. This is God's will for you. He wants you to keep coming to Him and sharing your heart with Him. The relationship is more important to God than just giving answers and direction. God wants you to walk in fellowship with Him each day. He is listening when you pray and He will answer when the time is right. The answers will come if we do not give up.

Be Steadfast

We must be steadfast in prayer to discover the will of God. Paul said, "pray without ceasing" (1 Thess 5:17). What does it mean? Can a man remain in the prayer closet all day and every day and never come out? Can a young mother remain in prayer without giving any attention to those children God has given her? The husband and wife who work to provide for the family can not possibly give themselves to prayer twenty-four seven, nor can the student who needs time to study, work, recreate, sleep, and be involved in extracurricular activities. How then can a believer be obedient to the command to "pray without ceasing?" Let the day begin with prayer and devotion to God. The first person we should speak with when we awaken is the Lord Jesus Christ. Daily devotion will lead to periods of private prayer. None of us can continually reside in a prayer closet, but we can commit ourselves to spend time in prayer and then walk in unbroken fellowship with the Lord throughout the day. Maturing in our relationship with Christ leads to the realization that we need to depend on the Lord at all times. Faithful followers of the Lord stay in touch with God. Daniel habitually prayed. He had a prayer schedule. He came to the private place of prayer three times each day to give thanks and make his petitions before God (Dan 6:10). Nehemiah prayed in preparation to return to Jerusalem and rebuild the walls of protection around the city and he depended on God in prayer throughout the rebuilding process (See Nehemiah 1). Paul, much like Jesus, made prayer a priority and instructed the saints to be devoted in prayer with thanksgiving (see Col 4:2). Prayer should become a way of life. God has promised in His Word that He will reveal His will to believers who continue in prayer. Jesus taught His disciples to continue to ask, seek, and knock: "Ask and it shall be given to you; seek and you will find; knock and it will be opened to you. For everyone who asks receives, and he who seeks finds, and to him who knocks it will be opened" (Matthew 7:7-8).

If we will begin the day devoted to the Lord in prayer, we will find ourselves praying as we walk, live, work, and play throughout the day. It will seem that we are praying all the time. We cannot spend all our time uttering prayers from our lips but we can practice the presence of God. It is possible to be in a spirit of prayer, realizing our complete dependence upon God to protect us, provide for us, and guide us. We can be conscious of His presence and yield ourselves to His will as He reveals it to us.

Steadfast prayer is fueled by fellowship with God. He is interested in being relational with us. If you find it difficult to abide in prayer it is likely because your focus is not on knowing God, but on getting something from Him. It is easy to look to God to discover His will and forget that what God wants most is a personal relationship. He desires for us to come to Him and spend time in fellowship with Him. God should not be treated like some online search engine which we only access to find the information we need about life. Christ is our life (Col 3:4). And through Him, God is redeeming mankind to walk in fellowship with Him and fulfill His purpose to His glory.

The need for prayer in the pursuit of God and His will is so vital that I have often asked other saints to pray on my behalf. Christians should pray for one another that all find what is pleasing to our Lord and live it out to His glory. Jesus prayed for all of His followers to be sanctified (vv.17-19), unified (vv.21-23), and glorified (vv.24-26). Paul prayed for the saints in the church at Thessalonica to become more and more like Christ and be "blameless" at the

Second Coming (1 Thess 5:23). A man named Epaphas prayed for his church, "always laboring fervently" for them in "prayers" that they may "stand perfect and complete in all the will of God"(Col 4:12-13). Let us pray, keep praying, and ask others to pray that we may clearly understand what the Spirit of God is leading us to do.

Be Sensitive to the Holy Spirit

Discovering the will of God is made possible by the Holy Spirit. He indwells to lead us into all truth (John 16:13-15). As we pray and read the Word of God, we should listen carefully to hear the Spirit speak. I will cover this subject in much more detail in the next chapter. Prayer leads to spiritual perception. We should believe God to answer the prayer for wisdom and direction (Jam 5:1-7).

Remember to rejoice. Be thankful. Keep praying. This is God's will in Christ Jesus for you. Do daily discipleship. Persevere in prayer. Spend quality time talking with the Lord and meditating on the Word. In His time, God will reveal His will to you. It will come gently into your heart, mind, and soul. You will begin to perceive and understand what God wants you to do.

CHAPTER FIVE

PERCEIVING GOD'S WILL

"Do not quench the Spirit. Do not despise prophecies."1 Thessalonians 5:19-20

I had been praying for quite some time about buying a new car. I needed a new car, but I could not afford one. The van that I had been driving was over fifteen years old, and I thought the transmission might be beginning to slip a little. I had a desperate need and all I knew to do was pray that God would show me what to do. The longer I prayed and read the Bible, the more I began to believe that God would somehow provide a new car for us. I was uneasy about driving the old van in its condition, but I simply could not afford to make another sizable monthly payment. As I prayed, I perceived in my heart that God was going to answer my prayer to meet this need, but I did not know how He would do it, or when. One morning as I was reading the Bible and praying about buying a new automobile I noticed that the word "inheritance" kept recurring. It seemed that every passage had something to do with receiving an inheritance. I understood this to be a promise from God that He would meet my need for transportation. I believe that the Lord was assuring me that He would show me His will. I thanked

God for His blessing ahead of time and told Him that I would wait for Him to act. In the meantime, I just kept driving that old van.

Prayer leads to spiritual perception. The saint who spends time praying for wisdom and direction will soon begin to discern the will of God. The Lord answered my prayer with a promise that He would meet my need for a new car. I would have preferred that God just appoint someone to buy it for me and leave it parked in my driveway. Instead, He had me waiting to see just how He would meet this need. I waited confidently and with peace in my heart because I knew that God had spoken to my spirit that my "inheritance" would come when the time was right.

God still speaks to His children today. People who desire to know His will should take time to listen and hear the still small voice of God. He keeps the lines of communication open with all of His children. It is a discipline true disciples must practice in order to keep walking in His will. Hearing God speak and obeying His voice is actually a principle taught in Scripture. Jesus said, "My sheep hear my voice, and I know them, and they follow Me" (John 10:27). The Holy Spirit works to guide believers into all the truth (John 16:13). Paul told the believers in the Church of Thessalonica to be careful not to "quench the Spirit" (1 Thess 5:19), nor "despise prophecies" (v. 20). These are two commands that Paul gives the church. "Do not quench the Spirit" is a negative command. No saint of God should ever quench the Holy Spirit. The Holy Spirit is like a fire in our hearts, and we should never "quench" or stifle His activity. Praying saints who walk in the Spirit should anticipate hearing from the Holy Spirit and obey His prompting.

One of the ways the Holy Spirit often worked in the early church was through the gift of prophecy. The cannon of Scripture (Bible) was not yet complete. The saints did not have copies of Scripture like we possess today. They often had to rely on God to speak and give direction though those who had the gift of prophecy. One would speak or "prophecy" and others with the gift of discernment would affirm or deny that the word was from God (see 1 Cor 14).

The point is to allow the Holy Spirit to speak and give direction. If you are praying for direction, does it not make sense that the Holy Spirit would begin moving to answer your prayer? God will reveal His mind to those who seek Him. I have learned that direction from the Lord usually comes to me through reading, studying, and meditating on Scripture, listening to the Spirit, considering my own desires, hearing from other saints, and taking note of my circumstances.

Direction often comes through the Scripture.

The primary way God directs His children is through the Bible. The first place to begin searching for the will of God is the inspired Word of God. Reading, meditating, learning, and applying the principles of the Bible will prepare the mind to discover what pleases God. All Scripture is inspired by God (2 Tim 3:16). Every word was written by men who were moved by God's Holy Spirit (2 Pet 1:20-21). Therefore, the Bible is not merely the work of man, but the work of God. The bible is God's book. If a person wants to know God's will about any matter, let him examine the sacred text of Scripture. A believer who knows and consistently applies the teaching of Scripture will be able to discern the will of God for her life (Rom 12:2).

God guides His children through the *Principles* from His Word. Many questions I receive from people about God's will are already answered in the Bible. I am not suggesting that the answer to every conceivable question is specifically spelled out in the texts, but I have found many answers to life's questions through the commands, precepts, and principles of the Bible. Many people struggle with understanding God's will because they are unlearned or uninterested in the teaching of Scripture. One lady came to my office years ago to talk about missions. She was not a member of my church, but I agreed to try and help her with the will of God for her life. She talked about how she knew God wanted her to do mission work, but she did not know where to start. I asked her, "Where do you attend church?" She said, "Oh, I don't attend church anywhere right now." I was totally dumbfounded. How could she be interested in missions and uninterested in the local church? It is God's will for every believer to be in fellowship with others believers in a local assembly (see Heb 10:24-25). In order to make disciples, we must be healthy disciples. I politely encouraged the dear lady to get involved in a local church before she thought anymore about missions.

As we read and meditate on the Bible, God will speak to guide us in His will. There is no better thing to do than read the Bible when you want to hear God speak to your heart. Absorbing God's Word into the mind will prepare our hearts to hear from God. There is a principle or a passage in the Bible that speaks to every issue in life. Do you have questions about relationships? The Bible gives wisdom. Spiritually speaking, the Bible says we should be equally joined. Light has no fellowship with darkness (see 2 Cor 6:14). Young people should chose their friends wisely because "Evil company corrupts good habits" (1Cor 15:33). Biblical principles should guide all relationships. Proper attitudes and respect between husbands and wives (Eph 5:21-33), parents and children (Eph 6:1-6), and employers and employees (Eph 6:5-9) are stated in the Word. Do you have questions about the will of God concerning finances? It is wise to study Bible passages that deal with money. The Bible speaks about hard work (Col 3:23-24). The Bible speaks about tithing (Mal 3:8-10) and giving to the work of God (Luke 6:38). The Bible warns of the dangers of borrowing and indebtedness (Prov 22:7). The Bible speaks to all of the issues of life. God's Word will guide believers along the right path (Psalm 119:105). Principles never fail.

God also guides through the *Promises* in His Word. The Lord will often show you a promise in His Word concerning the guidance for which you are asking Him. A promise that I have read in God's Word on many occasions is Psalm 32:8, *"I will instruct you and teach you in the way you should go; I will guide you with My eye."* Such promises assure us that God will show us what to do. When the living God makes a promise He always keeps it. The Lord may not always give us direction the moment we ask Him, but He is faithful to show us His will in His own time. In recent months we have been seeking the Lord in prayer about provision for our son's education. God has already provided much through grants, scholarships, and personal gifts. Today, we do not know where the remainder of the funds will come from, but we have the promises of God's Word to assure us that He is going to make a way for our son to complete his college education for the glory of God. The promises of God's provision are numerous in His Word. I often meditate on the following verses as I pray for provision:

> "And my God shall supply all of your need according to His riches in glory by Christ Jesus."
> - Philippians 4:19

> "The Lord is my shepherd; I shall not want."
> - Psalm 23:1

> "The young lions lack and suffer hunger; But those who seek the Lord shall not lack any good thing."
> - Psalm 34:10

> "Honor the Lord with your possessions, And with the firstfruits of all your increase; So your barns will be filled with plenty, And your vats will overflow with new wine."
> - Proverbs 3:9-10

When God shows you a promise in His Word, you can be sure that He is already at work in your life to answer your prayers and reveal His will to you.

God may, in a time of great need, guide with a *Personal Passage* in His Word. Have you ever read a passage of Scripture that seemed to address your personal questions or concerns? As we pray and meditate upon the Word, God will sometimes speak and give direction through a particular Bible verse that the Holy Spirit will single out and apply to our particular needs. This is always the exception and never the rule. We must be careful to habitually read and study Scripture passages in their original contexts and learn God's principles for the purpose of obeying them. It is dangerous to haphazardly flip through the Bible looking for some verse to affirm our own personal agendas. The will of God is about pleasing God, not about pleasing ourselves.

In college I had opportunity to begin preaching in a Baptist church near Bamberg, South Carolina. I preached for them each Sunday morning for about six weeks. I was not sure if they would ask me to become their pastor, but I wanted to be certain I was in the will of God. After several weeks of praying and asking God to show me His will about my life and this church, a particular passage of Scripture in the book of Acts captured my attention. Concerning Paul on mission, Luke wrote, "And a vision appeared to Paul in the night. A man of Macedonia stood and pleaded with him, saying, "come over to Macedonia and help us." Now after he had seen the vision, immediately we sought to go to Macedonia, concluding that the Lord had called us to preach the gospel to them" (Acts 16:9-10). In context, Paul needed direction and a call came through a vision of a man asking for help. I did not see a vision. I only read some Bible verses about a vision. The verses, however, were used of the Holy Spirit to show me the will of God concerning a call to this church. I concluded that God had called me to preach the gospel to them. If the church called me, I would accept the position. About a month later I received a phone call from a man in that little church. He informed me that the church wanted me to be their pastor. I accepted.

The Holy Spirit will sometimes speak through a Bible passage to guide a Spirit-filled believer who desperately wants to know which direction to go. Do you read the Bible daily? Keep reading and listening for God to speak to your heart. The Holy Spirit will do whatever necessary to assure you that you are walking in the will of God.

Direction may come directly from the Holy Spirit.

The Spirit of God lives in the hearts of the children of God. He speaks (Acts 13:2). He guides (John 16:13-15). He impresses the heart of believers to serve in particular ways. To refuse the prompting of the Holy Spirit is one way that we "quench" the Spirit (1Thess 5:19). We should walk in the Spirit (Gal 5:16) and follow His delicate whispering voice (see 1 Kings 19:12b). We should consistently pray for God's wisdom and listen to hear Him speaking. Hearing God is not like hearing a teacher with our literal ears. God speaks to the inner man. We hear the Lord with our spiritual ears (Rev 2:7,13,29; 3:6,13,22). The Spirit of God moves in the spirit of a child of God and gives quiet instruction.

I believe that the Holy Spirit has spoken to me, but most of the time He simply impresses my heart to do things or speak on a particular passage of Scripture. The Spirit brings thoughts into the minds of believers who seek the mind of God. This does not mean that every thought is from God. A person may have thoughts of suicide or murder. These kinds of thoughts are not from God but from the evil one (Eph 6:10-18). Some thoughts we have are selfish and self-serving. Impure motives can hinder our prayers and keep us from hearing God clearly (James 4:3). God speaks in such a way that believers know it is from the Spirit. I have learned through prayer and meditation on the Word to discern His prompting. I believe the more we read the Word and become familiar with the ways of God, the easier it becomes to know when Holy Spirit is dealing with us.

Direction may come from within one's own Self.

God sometimes places within our hearts what He wants us to do for Him. As we walk in fellowship with God, He gives us the desire to do something that will help others and bring glory to Him. This must be what King David had in mind as he wrote, "Delight thyself also in the Lord; and he shall give thee the desires of thine heart" (Psalm 37:4). When disciples of Jesus Christ desire to please Him, God is pleased to place within their hearts the desire to do something for the kingdom of God. Take time to look within. Think it over. Ask yourself, "what do I really want?"

Tim LaHaye contends that personal desires may be the first sign of the will of God for a devoted disciple. LaHaye says, "Don't be surprised if the first indication of God's will for you is your desire to do it. You may not identify it as a burden from the Lord or a witness of the Spirit, but that is exactly what it is. If a decision is biblically legitimate, it's probably God's will, as long as it does not violate you peace of heart."[13]

Our personal desires matter to God. He wants us to be satisfied in His will. He is not trying to make us unhappy. The will of God is a delight to those who are walking with the Lord (see Psalm 1). Spirit-filled believers who want to live a life pleasing to God will often know in their heart of hearts what God created them to be. God's purpose for our lives has been crafted to suit our own personality, talents, abilities, and gifts. It is okay to ask yourself what it is you would really like to happen in your own life. It is okay to dream of who and what you would like to become to the glory of God. I believe sometimes children have an inner notion of what they want to be and accomplish when they grow up. One child may say, "I want to be a fireman when I grow up." Another may say, "I am going to be a school teacher someday." The possibilities are limitless. The will of God is not always a new idea. It may be something that you have wanted all of your life. It is what you were created for. The will of God through the Lord Jesus Christ will give us a sense of belonging, peace, and purpose in life.

When a person is miserable in the will of God, it may be due to a bad attitude. Jonah rebelled against the will of God to go to Nineveh because he hated the Assyrians. Jonah did not delight in what pleased God. He had a wrong attitude. God loved the people of Nineveh and had mercy on them even though they were wicked. Jonah should have learned to love them as God did. When we love what God loves, we will begin to desire what He desires.

The penetrating examination of what you really believe, think, and desire may be an indication of the direction God wants you to go. Have you ever done any deep thinking or "soul-searching?" Have you ever had a feeling deep down in your soul about a person or thing that simply would not leave your thoughts? It may be that God planted that desire within your heart. It is certainly possible to have selfish and fleshly thoughts that are opposed to God's will, but often the saints who are walking with the Lord will desire in their hearts the very thing that God desires for them.

The consideration of the desires of our hearts is crucial in many areas. If a person is praying about getting married, it is certainly important that they desire to be with the other person. Why would God want you to marry someone that you do not like to spend time with? Do you really think that God wants you to spend the rest of your life with a person whom you find totally unattractive? Physical attraction is not of upmost importance, but it certainly matters. Character, godliness, and inner beauty matter most to God, but He will not pair you up with a person that you do not enjoy being with. God knows the desires of the heart in every area. If you are praying about your career choice, do you think God is going to make you do something for the rest of your life that you hate? There will be times when God calls us to serve Him in ways and in places that may not be to our particular liking, but He is not out to make us miserable. Our heart's desire should always be to obey the Lord regardless of what He requires.

Direction may come through the Saints in the local church.

God often speaks through other godly people. Paul warned the Thessalonians "do not despise prophecies"(1 Thess 5:20). God the Holy Spirit uses leaders and laity as well to speak for the purpose of edification (1 Cor 14:3). Pastors and teachers of God's Word are used by the Lord to give instruction (Eph 4:11). God holds each teacher accountable for their doctrinal integrity (James 3:1). Undershepherds, or pastors, are to be godly examples among the people and lead them to do God's will (1 Peter 5:1-5). Every Christian ought to be under the tutelage of Bible teachers in the local church (Heb 10:24-25). The truth of the Word renews the mind to discern what is pleasing to the Lord (Rom 12:2). God may use the words of the pastor's sermon to give direction for your life. It may be a Sunday School lesson that answers a question in a troubled heart. God may even burden another Christian to speak to you personally and give you some direction for your life. God often speaks though other Spirit-filled believers in the local church to give direction to a searching heart.

Think about it. The last person to encourage you to get involved in ministry may have been a spokesman from the Lord. I have been amazed at the people who have prayed for God to show them His will concerning a place of service and then turn down every invitation they have received to serve. The local church needs Sunday School teachers, small group leaders, help in the nursery, parking attendants, ushers, greeters, and a multitude of other ministries. God may be calling you to serve in some of these areas through an invitation of a Church leader, committee, or friend. Do not turn down personal invitations to serve, work, or go on mission too quickly. It may be the hand of God. The Lord may be speaking through them to call you to serve. Let us learn to listen to the godly people who God places in our lives.

GOD'S WILL for YOU

A word from the organist

Growing up as a PK (preacher's kid) presented many opportunities for mischief. One thing I would often do is walk by the organ and press some of the keys during the prelude to the evening worship service. The keys would stick and disrupt the play of the organist. I would make the most awful noises and then blame it all on Mrs. Cockrell. One Sunday evening as I passed by the organ on my mission of devilry, the saintly organist called me back. I just knew I had gotten on her last nerve. She asked me to sit with her for a minute. As she played she gave me a word of encouragement and wisdom concerning God's will for my life: "I heard you speak last Sunday morning, and I believe that God is calling you to preach." I thought the dear lady was losing her mind! I passed it off as nonsense. I did not think much more about what she said until the day I publically answered God's call in my life to preach the gospel almost a year later. After the announcement, she was first in line to speak to me. She looked directly into my eyes and said, "Now, what did I tell you?" God had actually used her to help chart a new course in my life. She planted a seed that God would use to confirm His call in my life. She saw something in me that I could not see. I suppose she heard me speak briefly on Student Sunday and discerned the gifting of the Holy Spirit in my life. Somehow God showed her that I would be a preacher and teacher of the gospel.

God will use our brothers and sisters in Christ to speak to us about His will for our lives. We must be sure that the person giving the advice is a godly Christian. Wisdom comes from a Spirit-filled follower of Jesus Christ. Some people think they can know the will of God for others when they themselves are not walking in the Spirit but according to the flesh. God does not want us to receive counsel from people who obviously are not walking in fellowship with Him. Listen to godly Christians who love the Lord and you.

Direction may come through circumstances.

God is Sovereign. He is in control of all things. The circumstances of life are sometimes an indicator of the hand of God. He opens and closes doors. An open door of opportunity that presents itself may be an indication of the will of God for you. An opportunity for promotion in the company may be the hand of God at work. The person you just met may have an impact on your future.

Paul could not go into several places to preach the gospel. He tried to get in, but the Holy Spirit would not let him. God closed a door. After some time, God spoke to him in a vision and Paul concluded that God wanted him to go on to Europe and preach the gospel there. It was the will of God. Paul obeyed (Acts 16:6-10). God may close a door that looks like a great opportunity. He will open another that is far better suited for the purpose and plan that He has for your life. Jesus said, "I have set before you an open door, and no one can shut it" (Rev 3:8b). God is in control. He is engineering our circumstances for the greater good (see Rom 8:28-29).

In 1989, one young lady tried to get into Carson Newman University to complete her education. This young lady had a beautiful voice and planned to sing with the school's Christian ensemble. She had friends there already, including her High School boyfriend. It looked like the perfect opportunity. She could be with her friends, sing, finish her degree, and be reunited with her "true love." She had her transcripts mailed two different times, but the school never received them. As a result, she could not transfer to that school. Needless to say, she was very disappointed. It was as if God was stopping her. Instead, she remained in South Carolina and enrolled at Charleston Southern University where she met a young ministerial student. She married him three years later. We have been married for over twenty years. God opens and closes doors of opportunity to help us understand and walk in His will.

Direction may not come immediately. God may not speak right away. Sometimes God is silent. Keep praying. God is teaching you to trust Him. He will show you step by step what He wants you to do.

CHAPTER SIX

PROVING GOD'S WILL

"Test all things. . ."1 Thessalonians 5:21a

In my own pursuit of the will of God I admit that often I fear doing the wrong thing. It is easy to be led astray. Many have taken what they believed to have been a "leap of faith" in God's will that turned out to be a leap of foolishness. How can a believer avoid being deceived and making a mistake? Who knows which option is best? Can a person really be sure that the "vision" in mind is indeed the will of God?

Vance Havner compared false teachers and preachers to an old clock in his home. Havner said the old clock had been stored in the attic because it no longer worked. It had not kept time in years. He called it an old dead clock. Havner pointed out that even though the hands on that clock never moved, it still displayed the correct time twice a day, every day! Even a spiritually dead man can pass along some sound doctrine. The devil's advocates often include just enough of the truth of God's Word in their presentations to make their erroneous messages seem acceptable. It is all based on lies, but it sounds good. The practice is nothing new. The devil has been using the same strategy since the Garden of Eden (see Gen 3).

The Bible says, "Test all things"(1 Thess 5:21). I find it very interesting that Paul was led by the Holy Spirit to give a command to "test all things" immediately following a clear mandate to pay careful attention to prophecies. Why would he do it? It seems counterproductive. He tells them to listen to the preaching but not be too quick to believe it. Actually, it is very sound advice.

Testing spiritual proclamations was very important in the early days of Christianity. All kinds of false prophets were at work. Believers could not simply accept everything they heard. They had to listen with a critical ear and be discerning. They had to examine all teaching and prophetic words to be certain that it was coming from God. The same is true for believers today.

We must always "test the spirits" (see 1 John 4:1). Every thought we have will not be from above (James 3:15). Advice coming from others, even though they may have good intentions, will not always be from the Lord. We must test every thought, vision, word, or idea to be certain that we are hearing from God and obeying His will. We live in an "evil" day (Eph 5:16). It is easy for us to be deceived by someone claiming to have a message from God. To "prove" or test a thought, word, idea, or vision that we believe we have received from God is a process of allowing the Holy Spirit to sift our thinking and check our motives to be sure they are pure. There are things you may not know about the people whom you are joining in a business venture. There may be information unavailable to you that would change the way you look at opportunities or invitations. The great news is that God knows all things and He is willing to protect His children from deception. I suggest three ways to test the thought, word, idea, or vision that we may think is from God: (1) The Principle test of God's Word, (2) The Peace test from the indwelling Spirit, and (3) The Practical test of wisdom.

The Principle Test

First, we should always test every thought, idea, and vision by **God's Word.** I call this the "principle test." The Bible is the will of God in print. It is inerrant and infallible. There is no way to go wrong obeying the principles of Scripture. God's Word is the standard for Christian living. Any violation of the teaching of Scripture is a step away from the perfect will of God. The Lord will never lead any of His children to do anything contrary to what is taught in the Bible. The Word is like a measuring stick. If our thoughts, ideas, or vision do not measure up to the standard of the Word of God, then we know it is not His will.

In the late 70's the Carowinds amusement park opened near Charlotte, North Carolina. It was only about an hour away from our home in Lancaster, South Carolina. We loaded the church bus and arrived before the park opened. I wanted to try everything! I remember how frustrated I became when I was not allowed to board certain amusements. At the entrance of each ride was an attendant with a measuring stick. The children that did not measure up to the predetermined mark did not get to ride. It was all about safety. The standard was established to protect smaller children from accidental injury. The Bible is God's primary measuring tool. God has His standards set in His Word to protect His children. He knows best. To take a "ride" that has been forbidden by the Word of the Lord is foolish and dangerous. The ride may look like loads of fun and many people may be jumping on board for a momentary thrill, but a child of God has to refuse what is forbidden by the Word. Our loving Heavenly Father has set standards to protect us. Never do anything contrary to the teaching of Scripture. God's will is always in harmony with His Word. The devil tempts us to ignore the principles of Scripture in decision making. Often Christians "pray about" things without considering what the Bible teaches. To pray and decide without meditating on Scripture is like cooking without a recipe. It's all guess work. God does not want His children guessing about His plans. The Bible is God's guidebook for life.

Many questions about what pleases God have already been settled for us in the Word. One man came to his pastor and claimed that God had revealed to him that he should divorce his wife and mother of his children and marry a more "spiritual" woman. The pastor lovingly reminded the man that the Bible states that "God hates divorce" (Mal 2:16) and that from creation He designed a man to be joined to his wife for life (Gen 2:24; Matt 19:1-12). This man who wanted to leave his wife and family for another woman was not hearing from God. He was simply caving into his own fleshly desires. God will never direct anyone to do anything that is contrary to the written Word. Before any child of God makes any decision in life, he should be sure that it is consistent with the teaching of Scripture.

The Peace Test

Second, we should test our every thought, idea, and vision by **God's peace**. Paul prayed for the Thessalonian believers that the "God of peace" would sanctify them perfectly (1 Thess 5:23). God is the God of peace and those who follow Jesus wholeheartedly will experience an abiding peace which "surpasses all understanding"(see Phil 4:7). If a saint is not experiencing the peace of God in his heart, something is wrong. The absence of peace is a warning from the Holy Spirit of God that the decision you are making is the wrong one. The peace of God is a sense of contentment within the heart. The Holy Spirit graces us with a settled spirit when things are in harmony with the will of God. When a child of God walks in the will of God he will experience God's peace within. The opposite of peace is a restless, uncomfortable, check in the human spirit. Some call it a "red flag." Something is just not right. The more we pray and meditate on God's Word the more we become convinced that we may be about to make a mistake. This is when a follower of

Christ needs to wait and reevaluate. The absence of God's peace is a sign from God that we should not move forward with our plans because He has something better in mind. To move ahead without experiencing peace from God is foolish. God suspends peace to keep us from getting out of His will.

One example

When we first moved to Southwestern Baptist Theological Seminary in Fort Worth, Texas, my wife and I needed work. I had been pastor of a small church while I was in college, and I thought the Lord may bless me with a pastorate in seminary. After just two weeks of praying, a door came open. A new church plant in South Texas was looking for a pastor. They asked me to come and fill the pulpit several Sunday mornings. After several weeks, the pastor search committee asked me to come preach in view of a call. They believed it was God's will for me to become their pastor. I agreed to come back the very next Sunday. The church made plans to vote on me after the morning message.

We went back to Fort Worth that afternoon thinking it was all but done. All I had to do was come back the next Sunday with a good message and I would be the pastor. The church was over a hundred miles from the seminary, but they were going to provide housing on a lake. We could drive down on a Friday and stay until after the evening service on Sunday. It all sounded great. Back at home I began reading my Bible and working on a message for the big day. I studied and prayed for about two days and realized that I was not making much progress. I became troubled in my spirit. It was like a mental blockage. I was not getting a message to preach. It was as if God was telling me that something was not right. The longer I prayed, the more I became convinced that I should not accept a call to this church. I told the Lord I would only do what He gave me peace about doing. I did not understand why God would not allow me to accept a call from this church, but without a sense of peace from Him, I knew it was the wrong thing to do. Once I made this commitment to do the will of God, I returned to sermon preparation and finished the message for Sunday with little difficulty.

We began our long journey to that church on Sunday morning. Along the way, I told my wife about the absence of peace from God. She was quite surprised. We had no steady income at the time. The savings account was running very low. All we could do was trust God to give us other opportunities if He was closing this door. We agreed that I would tell the church that morning that I had no peace from God about becoming their new pastor. After I preached the morning message, I asked permission to speak to the congregation before they voted. I said, "You all need to know that I have been praying fervently about becoming your pastor, but I have no peace from God about accepting a call to this fine church." I assured them that I had no problem with anyone or anything in their fellowship. I simply had no peace about becoming their pastor. We returned to Fort Worth assured that we did the right thing. About two months later we discovered that my wife was pregnant with our first son, Austin. She was often so sick that she couldn't even attend church on Sunday in Fort Worth. If I had taken that church, which was over a hundred miles away from the seminary, she would not have been able to travel on weekends. Six months after Austin was born God gave us a church in East Texas. The people provided a house to live in right next to the church. We moved away to that field of ministry. It was a practical choice. I commuted to classes until I graduated. It was far better on my wife and infant son. It was worth the wait. It was God's will for us. If you have not peace, do not proceed.

The Practical Test

*Third, we should test our every thought, idea, and vision with **God's wisdom**.* I call this application of wisdom the "practical test." This is the test where all the information of the decision you are making is brought together for consideration. The information is processed and a practical solution surfaces. The pursuit of the will of God is not a mindless exercise. God grants wisdom as we use our minds to evaluate all things under the guidance of the Holy Spirit. Without Spiritual wisdom the child of God would never make progress in discovering God's will (see 1 Cor 2:12-16). I personally believe the will of God to be very practical. I know the will of God does not always make sense to us because we do not always see things the way God sees them. He knows all things. When we all get to heaven we will be amazed at how God put everything together perfectly. I may not understand why God allows certain things to happen on earth, but I know He can be trusted to work all things together for good for those of us who love Him and are the called according to His purpose (see Rom 8:28-29).

What is wisdom?

Wisdom is properly applying knowledge. The Bible says that "wisdom is the principle thing" (Proverbs 4:7). Wise living is always the will of God for His children. As Christians, to walk in wisdom is to apply the knowledge of the truth of God's Word to our daily lives. Wisdom gives us God's perspective. By wisdom we see things the way God sees them. It takes wisdom to know God's will. The Bible instructs believers who lack wisdom to ask. James says, "If any of you lacks wisdom, let him ask of God, who gives to all liberally and without reproach, and it will be given to him" (James 1:5).

Again we see the principle of persistent prayer in discerning the will of God. If you are not yet seeing your way clearly, just continue to pray and seek the truth. Keep asking God for wisdom. Study the issues surrounding the decision you must make. Ask lots of questions. Gather as much information as you possibly can and continue to pray. God will give you wisdom to apply knowledge and make the best of choices. Wisdom will give the saints a clearer understanding of what would be pleasing to the Lord in their particular circumstances. It keeps us out of trouble. Wisdom will let us know when we are about to take a "leap of foolishness" instead of a "leap of faith."

Hogs or no hogs?

When I was pastor of Aynor First Baptist Church, I was approached by a man who was considering going into a new business. He had been a crop farmer for years, but he saw an opportunity to do something new and exciting- raising hogs! This man came to my office again and again to discuss the possibility of this new and exciting business venture. I must admit that in the beginning I had my doubts about the vision, but the longer I listened to my friend talk about hog farming, the more convinced I became that his notion may be God's will for him. In our discussions we talked about the practicality of his idea. Was there a market for hogs? Did this man have the ability, resources, and know-how to manage a hog raising operation? Was this man willing to endure the stench? Was his wife okay with all of this? In the sessions, I would ask the questions and just sit and listen to this farmer talk. I knew him well enough to know he was not one to jump into anything fanciful. He was frugal. He tithed his income in the local church. He believed in hard work, and he knew how much demanding labor his new business may require. He was ready and willing to do whatever it took to get it going and keep it going. I was also impressed by the fact that he continued to pray and seek my advice about understanding the will of the Lord. He really wanted God's will for his life. All things considered, I could find no good reason for this man to stay away from the swine. I told him to keep praying and do what he thought the Lord was leading him to do. I was confident that he would be successful if he pursued his vision. A few months later he was raising hogs by the hundreds. That was over ten years ago. As far as I know, the hog farm is still going strong.

I share the story for several reasons. First, God is interested in you and your life no matter who you may be. He has a purpose for farmers just as He does for doctors, school teachers, mangers, salesman, machinists, mechanics, businessmen, preachers, or whomever. The Lord is not partial. He is concerned with whatever concerns you. I also share this story as an example of how *practical* I believe the will of God to be. God's wisdom will shed light on the practicality of what He is calling you to do for Him. I know some will disagree that God's will is practical and that it often makes no sense. I agree that the will of God can at times be mystifying and perplexing. However, I am convinced that even when the will of God makes no sense to us, it makes perfect sense to Him. If we could only see things from God's perspective. That is what wisdom is. We see things the way God the Father sees them. Pray for God to give you wisdom and you will better understand what God wants you to do and why He wants you to do it.

Looking back, I thought my calling to preach and teach the gospel made no sense at all. I needed education. I had very little money. And I did not think I could prepare sermons and stand up and preach for thirty or forty minutes at a time. Today, I know better. It was the right thing for me all along. God called and gifted me to be a pastor-teacher. Therefore, going into the ministry was the most practical thing I could have done with my life. It made no sense at the time. In retrospect, it was one of the best decisions I have ever made.

Application

Let us attempt to walk through the process of getting wisdom and applying it to our pursuit of God's will. To help us apply wisdom in the process of discovering God's will we look to the Apostle Paul's letter to the Ephesians:

> "See then that you walk circumspectly, not as fools
> but as wise, redeeming the time, because the days
> are evil. Therefore do not be unwise, but understand
> what the will of the Lord is."
>
> -Ephesians 5:15-17

Wisdom is intrinsical with the will of God. To walk in wisdom is to take a path that will surely lead to God's will for your life. Paul's teaching in wise walking can be applied by obeying three principles for living in an "evil" day (v.16). God's wisdom will lead believers to:

- Be prudent - Examine all things carefully (v.15).
- Be proactive - Make the most of the time (v.16).
- Be perceptive - "Understand the will of the Lord" (v.17)

Wisdom will make believers *prudent* in their walk with the Lord. To walk in wisdom we must first "walk circumspectly"(v.15, NKJV), or watch out and be careful as we take each step. Because "the days are evil" (v.16b), we must be cautious and examine everything carefully. Every step should be one of obedience in the will of God. Our desire is to do whatever pleases Him. Therefore, the daily intake of God's Word is essential to discovering the will of God (Rom 12:2). The truth of God is paramount in every aspect of life.

But to be careful to make wise decisions we should also acquire as much useable information as possible about every invitation, opportunity, vision, or idea and make careful inspection. The wise person knows the value of gaining knowledge: "The heart of the prudent acquires knowledge, and the ear of the wise seeks knowledge" (Proverbs 18:15). Uninformed decisions are usually bad decisions. It is wise to get all the facts and figures. Ask lots of questions. Seek godly counsel. Read books and articles about the subject matter. In our information age, via the internet, we can access an immeasurable amount of knowledge about almost any subject. The time invested in the inquiry, analysis, and reflection is time well spent.

The believer who is prudent to study the issues will also be *proactive*. To walk in God's wisdom is to work diligently. The wise person will be proactive and seek out the needed information without delay. The Bible says that we should always be "redeeming the time"(v.17). To redeem the time is to buy it up and make the most of it. Believers should never waist time. Every moment is precious because life passes so quickly (James 4:14). How are you spending your time? Taking the time to investigate, analyze, and reflect upon the findings before making decisions is obeying the command to make the most of time. If you are meditating on the Word and praying about the will of God for your life, you are wise. If you are taking time to analyze life's choices according to Scripture, you will find that foolishness is far from you. If you are daily serving the Lord to do what you know is right, you can be confident that He will show you the next step in His plan for your life. To be on the alert to process knowledge about your particular calling, vocation, project, ministry, or whatever it is that you are currently considering, is key to realizing God's will for you.

The prudent and proactive disciple who seeks the Lord and studies the issues will soon begin to perceive the will of the Lord. The Bible commands believers to "understand" God's will (v.17). It will become clear in our hearts and minds. With the help of the Holy Spirit, we can prayerfully process the information that we have gathered and discern what God would have us to do. Often, the solution to the problem will present itself. Lost people make major decisions based only on the limited information they have acquired, but spiritually minded believers will evaluate all things in fellowship with God. All the information is pulled together and scrutinized in the light of His Word. The Holy Spirit will show us what is best. It is wise to lay everything before the Lord and ask Him to reveal His point of view. Heaven's perspective is essential to discovering and doing what is best for everyone involved.

Troubled Tommy

Tommy had prayed for a new job for months. He had advanced in his company and his salary kept him and his family comfortable, but he desired to do more. He wanted the best for his family and thought if he could land a job with a larger salary, it would be better for all of them. He really believed God would bless him with a new opportunity. The opportunity came. It all looked good on paper. Tommy would have the position that he wanted and the salary to go along with it. Most people would have leaped without a second thought.

Tommy decided to pray about it. He wisely began to meditate on God's Word and examine all things carefully. Tommy began to realize that taking the new job would mean that he would be away from home a lot. The precious time he had been spending with his teenage daughter would be reduced to weekends. He was already aware of the battle she was having with her own self-image and some peer pressure, and he had been spending more time with her to help with the struggles. In addition, he also considered the current state of his marriage and he was concerned that his wife may not be able to handle such dramatic change easily. After praying over all the information he chose *not* to accept the new position. The family was more important than the extra money. The current state of affairs convinced him that a change may make a difficult situation at home worse. Tommy really wanted the job and the money, but it was simply unwise for him to be away from his wife and daughter at that particular time in their lives. Tommy said "no." It was a wise choice. It was the will of God.

Father knows best

There are times when God's will does not make any sense to us. It may *seem* very impractical. God's will for you may even look impossible and make no sense at all from man's perspective. Let us remember that when things make no sense to us it may due to the fact that our knowledge is limited. We do not always see everything clearly, but we can be confident that God knows what He is doing. God requires His children to have faith (see Heb 11:6). We simply cannot know *all* of the information nor what lies ahead, but God knows all things and He knows what is best. He often tests our faith. Abraham chose to obey by faith when he was told to go out and he did not know where he was going (Genesis 12:1). God also told him to sacrifice his own son in worship (Genesis 22:19). Why would God tell him to sacrifice the son He had given through whom all his decedents would come? It just did not make any sense. Noah was commanded to build an ark without a body of water anywhere nearby. He must have looked stupid in the eyes of his neighbors. God had purpose in telling Abraham and Noah to do things that did not make any sense at the time they received the command. It made sense in heaven, but they could not have fully understood how God would work it all out on earth. Looking back on it now we can see that God's will made perfect sense. God knew what He was doing all along. We must trust Him when we do not understand why He leads us to take some challenges that seem impossible and ridiculous from a human perspective. Do not be surprised if God leads you to do something that causes others to think you are foolish. It is only foolish to live outside of the will of God. Just obey the voice of the Lord. If God tells you to change jobs, buy or sell property, start a church, or go out and buy an ice cream truck and start selling ice cream then I say, "Do it for the glory of God." However, be sure that you have spent time in prayer and communion with God in His Word. Always do what God leads you to do. You will be glad that you did.

What about that new car?

Having evaluated the facts and figures, we concluded that we could not afford another car payment. The burden would be too heavy to bear. To borrow more money, from our perspective, would have been foolish (Rom 13:8). I am not always opposed to borrowing, but I knew to go even further into debt would mean that my family would be even more enslaved (Prov 22:7). I am sure that sometimes people, perhaps even in my own church, wanted to ask, "Pastor, why do you continue to drive that piece of junk?" My answer: I am waiting on God's very best. He had shown me His promise in His Word. I had faith that my "inheritance" would come in His perfect time. With no possibility of any new transportation in sight, I asked God to help me be content with the old van until He blessed us with another automobile.

CHAPTER SEVEN

POSSESSING GOD'S WILL

". . . hold fast that which is good."1 Thessalonians 5:21b

It was my first trip to the plate as a young ball player. I had
dreamed of hitting the ball over the center field fence, but at this
point I would have settled for a base on balls. It only took three
pitches. I stood at the plate and watched all three whizz by me. All
called strikes. Let's just say, it did not work out like I had planned. As
I left the batter's box and walked slowly back to the bench with my
head down, coach Connell met me with a gentle reminder: "Rookie,
if you want to hit the ball you must swing the bat." The knowledge
of the will of God is only knowledge until we apply it. At some point
God's people have to step up to the plate and swing the bat. God
will open doors for His children to walk in His will. We should not
disregard them or stand still and watch opportunity pass. Now that
we know what God wants us to do, it is time to do it. It is time to
possess our possessions. It is time to take action. We must seize the
divine opportunity before it passes.

The Bible says, "hold fast that which is good" (1 Thess 5:21b)
which means to remember and hold to the truth and live by it. It is
never enough for the saints to know the Word of God, we must obey

it (James 1:22). Once we know the truth we should hold tightly to it, remember it, and apply it. Likewise, when God has spoken and revealed His will we must do it. God shows us His will so that we will obey it.

The children of Israel had been led to the promise land with the assurance that God would give it to them. Joshua, by faith, led the troops into battle to conquer. God had already promised them the land, but now they had to go in and possess it. Joshua told them they must go in and possess what God had given them (see Joshua 1:10-11). The same is true for a believer who wants to live in the center of God's will. God reveals His will at the right time and calls His children to go in and take ownership!

We Possess the will of God by Faith

The path of the will of God has already been laid out before us but, by faith, we must take the path and complete the journey. Faith is paramount. In fact, because faith is so vital in finding God's will I have devoted an entire chapter to it (see pp. 72). When God shows us what He desires for us in life, it is our responsibility to Trust Him and do it.

Every step in the will of God is to be taken by faith. Salvation is by faith (Jn 3:16). A person is saved the moment they place their faith in the crucified, buried, and risen Son of God (Rom 10:9-10,13). The atoning death of Christ is sufficient. True Believers can be confident that all sin is washed away and heaven is a certainty from the very moment they trust in Christ as Lord and Savior. Just as we have trusted Christ to save, we must trust Him to show us His will and to empower us to do it. Without faith it impossible to please God (Heb 11:1-6).

Moses, by faith, raised his rod at the Red sea and the waters parted for the People of God to crossover. The Egyptians, who had no faith, attempted to cross but were "swallowed up"(Heb 11:29). No one can accomplish the will of God without faith. Peter walked across the water at Jesus command but began to sink when he doubted (Matt 14:22-33). He did the impossible by faith and only failed when he doubted. Faith is essential to doing God's will.

All of the saints we read about in the book of Hebrews, chapter eleven, faced great challenges, but they all obeyed the will of God by faith. Fear keeps many people from obeying the Lord. They know God's will but, out of fear, they refuse to do it. What God is calling you to do may be a tremendous challenge. The will of the Lord is not always easy, but nothing is too difficult with God. He can handle anything. Goliath was much bigger and stronger than David, but God enabled David to kill the giant and cut off his head (1 Sam 17). Daniel was no match for those hungry lions, but God closed their mouths and delivered Him safely (Daniel 6). Jesus accepted the Father's will for Him and went to the cross and died for our sins, and God raised Him up and exalted Him to the highest place (Phil 2:5-11). No matter what we face in His will, God is up to the challenge. "He who calls you is faithful and He will also do it"(1 Thess 5:24).

We Possess the will of God in the power of the Holy Spirit

The Holy Spirit is the power of God within to enable believers to understand and accomplish God's will. It is not personal strength and ability, but the power of the Spirit, that enables people to do great things for God (Zech 4:6).

The Spirit guides and teaches truth to make followers of Christ more and more like Him as they hear and obey the word of God and walk in the will of God (John 14:26; 16:13-14). He empowers believers to be witnesses for Christ (Acts 1:8). He also strengthens the saints as they employ their spiritual gifts in service to others (1 Peter 4:10-11). All of the will of God is to be carried out in the power of Christ who pours His power through His servants (Phil 4:13). Every child of God is responsible to be filled with the Spirit (Eph 5:18), and to walk in the Spirit (Gal 5:16).

We must Possess the will of God and persevere in it

Perseverance is crucial. It is easy to get discouraged. The devil will tempt a willing servant of Christ to give up and quit before the task is complete. Our adversary, the devil, prowls about like a roaring lion seeking whom he may devour"(1 Peter 5:8-9). Paul encouraged the believers in the churches in Galatia to keep working until they reaped a spiritual harvest: "And let us not grow weary while doing good, for in due season we shall reap if we do not loose heart"(Galatians 6:9).

A new believer set out to win his lost friend to Christ. He invited him to church and offered to give him a ride to Sunday School. The friend agreed to attend the next Sunday. When he arrived to pick up his friend he knocked on the front door but got no response. Everyone in the house was still asleep. Instead of giving up, the determined disciple decided to get his friend out of bed. He found a ladder on the front lawn, leaned it up against the house, climbed to the second level, and tapped on the bedroom window. He was successful. The friend quickly dressed and made it to church. The gospel was preached. The boy was saved. A month later he was baptized. Never give up!

We must Possess the will of God to the Glory of God

Why are you pursuing this thought, idea, and vision? I it for your glory or the Lord's? Mankind should glory in nothing but the cross of Christ (Gal 6:14). God should receive all the glory for all we accomplish (1 Cor 10:31). Without Him our ministries would be fruitless and useless (see John 15).

In June, 2012, Dr. Fred Luter was elected as the new president of the Southern Baptist Convention. He was the first African American to hold that position. When he came to the microphone to speak, he made one simple statement: "To God be the glory for the things He has done." Well said. All things should be done to bring glory to God.

Did I get the car?

Six months passed with nothing new to drive. In the process of praying about our need for a new "ride," my wife concluded that the Lord wanted her to go back to work (part-time) as a substitute teacher in the local elementary school where our daughter Megan attends. She liked the idea because she could go with Megan to school each morning and come home again with her in the afternoon. It was perfect. She could serve others, get paid, and never miss anything at home. We also decided to add most of her earnings to our savings account in order to buy our next car. According to our calculations, in a year's time we would have enough money to trade for a newer car. This was God's will for us. In answer to our prayers, He gave greater opportunity to serve and the increased income that we needed. In the process, of course, we were able to give more to the local church. As I reflected on how God was working in our lives, a principle of Scripture came to mind:

> "Let him who stole steal no longer, but rather *let him labor*, working with his hands what is good, that he may have something to give him who has need."
> -Ephesians 4:28

God wants His children to work hard, save some, and give some away. It's the duty of every disciple. God works in our lives when we obey the principles in His Word. To Him be the glory!

Still Searching?

If you have not yet discovered God's will for your life, just persevere. Keep praying and walking with the Lord and, in His time, He will show you what to do. Devoted discipleship will certainly lead to discovery. It is easy to have a faith shortage sometimes. If you are having doubts that you will ever clearly understand God's plans for your life, fear not, God is likely testing your faith (James 1:2-7). He desires your faith to grow stronger in the process. Is our faith as strong as God wants it to be? We will consider this question of faith in the next chapter.

CHAPTER EIGHT

THE WILL OF GOD AND FAITH

"But without faith it is impossible to please Him, for he who comes to God must believe that He is, and that He is a rewarder of those who diligently seek Him." Hebrews 11:6

Several years ago our family made our first trip to Disney World in Orlando, Florida. It was an adventure we had anticipated for months. I had never seen our children so excited. When the day finally arrived, we stood in front of Family Kingdom and looked through the gates at all the wonder that awaited us. We quickly pulled our park passes from a special handbag where my wife had secured them. If we were to experience all the magic of Walt's wonderful world, we had to be admitted to the park. Up to that moment, we were only on the outside looking in. We had envisioned ourselves in the midst of all the excitement and wonder, but we knew it was only a vision until we actually passed through the gates and into the place where "dreams come true."

Many Christians believe that God has a plan for their lives and that a great adventure awaits them, but they do not know how to access it. They are only on the outside looking in. Faith is our pass into the great adventure of God's will. Without faith, we never get beyond planning, envisioning, and dreaming of the wonderful plans that God has made for us.

Faith is Essential

In the last chapter I stated that we should possess or do the will of God by faith. Without faith we cannot in any way please God (Heb 11:6). Why have we not yet discovered God's personal plan? We have prayed, meditated on the Word, studied the issues, and received godly counsel from others and yet we are still uncertain of the path that God would have us to follow. Could we have a problem with faith? Are we confident that God is hearing us as we pray for wisdom (see James 1:5-7)? Do we wait with the assurance that God is going to be true to His Word and show us His purpose and plan for our lives? Let's be honest. If we must answer "no" to any of these questions we may have a faith problem. A lack of faith hinders discovery. No one can discover and do the will of God without faith. To do the will of God is to please God, so faith is required of those who desire to be obedient to His will.

The author of Hebrews candidly states the essentiality of faith. He asserts that without faith it is "impossible" to please God (11:6a). Doubt never pleases the Lord. Unbelief is never God's will for anyone. God hears and answers the prayer of the saint who comes to Him in faith asking for wisdom "without any doubting" (James 1:5-8). The exciting pathway of discovering the will of God is certainly a journey of trusting in the Lord wholeheartedly (Proverbs 3:5-6). In pursuit of the will of God, we must believe that God is who He says He is and that He will reward us with wisdom and insight if we will "diligently seek Him"(Hebrews 11:6b). Those who have faith in God and seek Him will be blessed with the knowledge of His will.

Faith Explained

What is faith? If discovering and doing the will of God requires faith, then all who desire to know and do His will must understand the concept. The author of Hebrews provides a profound description: "Now faith is the substance of things hoped for, the evidence of things not seen"(Hebrews 11:1). The word "faith" carries the idea of *trust* in God and *dependence* upon Him to act on behalf of one who looks to Him for help. To have faith is to take God at His Word. It is to take action because we are confident that God is going to take action based on His promises. If God has made a promise, then He will certainly keep it. It's really that simple. I love the *Faith* acrostic:

Forsaking
All
I
Trust
Him

The book of Hebrews speaks of many men and women of faith who took God at His word and lived according to His will. We will examine the lives of the faithful later in this chapter to see how God worked through them to accomplish what seemed unlikely and often impossible. The will of God is certainly impossible for man to accomplish alone, but with God "All things are possible" (Matt 19:26).

A Closer Look

It will help to break down the description of Faith in Hebrews 11:1. The text gives two characteristics about faith: (1) Faith is the substance of things hoped for. (2) Faith is the evidence of things not seen.

The author of Hebrews expresses the true nature of faith. He knew that God could be trusted to accomplish His supernatural works through a willing servant who seeks to do His will for His glory. To help his readers mature in the faith, the author of Hebrews was led by the Holy Spirit to deliver a fascinating and insightful description of what it means to trust in the Lord.

First, "faith is the substance of things hoped for" (11:1a). What does it mean to "hope" for something? Hope is not wishful thinking. We often use the word hope to convey our wishes. "I hope we have chicken for dinner." "I hope it snows." "I hope the Dallas Cowboys win the Super Bowl this year."(Now that is wishful thinking!). Biblical hope is not like that. Hope in the Bible is a confident expectation. To hope is to be certain. What enables the saints to realize this hope that we have? Faith! Because of our faith in the Lord God, the things hoped for are things that are certain to come. Faith is the "substance" or foundation of hope. "Faith is the basis, the substructure (*hypostasis* means lit. "that which stands under") of all that the Christian life means, all that the Christian hopes for."[14] What makes hope a reality? Faith. Our faith in Christ assures us that whatever God promises He will do. God always keeps His promises. He may delay in keeping them. Often he requires the saints to wait upon Him. Like many of the faithful who have gone before us, we may not live to see every promise of God fulfilled, but we know for certain that God is faithful to keep His Word in His perfect timing.

Faith is also the "evidence of things not seen"(11:1b). This statement is similar in meaning to the first. The meaning of the word "evidence" is the same as "confidence" (NASB) or to be "certain" (NIV). By faith in Christ Jesus we are certain of many invisible realities. The author of Hebrews was certain of God's creative handiwork even though he was not present when God created everything out of nothing: "By faith we understand that the worlds were framed by the word of God, so that the things which are seen were not made of things which are visible" (Hebrews 11:3). God actually made everything out of nothing. God did it. No human being saw Him do it but, by faith, we are certain that by God's Word all of creation came into existence (see also Gen 1,2). How do we know that God created the universe? The Bible tells us in the first verse of Genesis: "In the beginning God created the heavens and the earth"(1:1). Christians are creationists, not evolutionists. We are confident that God created it all by faith.

By faith we can also discern and do the will of God if we seek Him earnestly. By faith we can understand and envision the life that God wants us to lead. By faith we can "venture into the future" on the basis of God's Word alone.[15] God will show His children what He wants them to accomplish in life and by faith they can reach out into the future and grasp the concept of it. The will of God for you may be a mystery at the moment, but by faith, it will soon be a way of life. We must learn to trust Him to show us His will.

Easier said than done

Learning to trust God and to take Him at His Word may be quite a challenge. It is a process. We must grow in our faith in God the Father. When our boys were toddlers I loved to stand them up on the counter top in the kitchen or up on the hood of the car and say, "Jump!" I vividly remember the uncertainty in the eyes of our oldest son the first time I tested him. He hesitated for a moment and then he leaped into my arms. To his delight, and mine, I did not drop him. God the Father cannot fail. He wants us to know that He is God and He can and should be trusted to catch us every time we act on faith. The better we get to know Him, the more we will trust Him. Once a child learns that Dad is trustworthy, he or she will begin leaping off the top of everything expecting the hands of a loving father to catch them.

Is this a blind leap of faith? No. I did not ask my son to jump off the car and into the dark. I asked him to jump off the car into my arms. God is a loving and trustworthy Father who calls us to leap into His arms, in the name of Jesus Christ, and trust Him to save us, provide for us, deliver us, and to accomplish His will through us. The Bible gives many examples of men and women who trusted God and obeyed Him. It would help to examine some of the faithful.

Faith Exemplified

Hebrews 11 recalls many of heroes of the Faith who were called to do the will of God and exercised faith in God to obey Him. They heard the Word of God and obeyed. It pleases God for His children to live by faith and obey Him. This is God's will for you.

Abel obeyed God by faith. The command was simple. Bring the proper blood sacrifice and worship. Every disciple of Jesus Christ should worship God "in spirit and in truth" (John 4:24). This is the will of God. Abel had no idea that his act of faith and obedience would cost him his life. Cain, his own brother, out of jealousy and anger rose up and killed him. Cain refused to accept the fact that his sacrifice was unacceptable. He also refused to deal with his anger which opened the door to murder (see Gen 4:7-8). Cain let one sin lead to another. Instead of repenting and returning to make things right, he allowed his fleshly desires to get the best of him and he took it out on his brother. Abel did the right thing by worshiping according to the Word. He trusted God. He obeyed God. He did the will of God. Abel was the first one to do the will of God and suffer persecution (see 2 Tim 3:12).

Enoch walked with God. He understood that to be in fellowship with God was the will of God for his life. Every disciple of Jesus Christ should have an intimate walk with Him. Enoch walked so closely and intimately with God that "He took him." One day as Enoch walked along in fellowship with God, he was translated. He was taken from earth up into heaven. In the twinkling of an eye, he was gone. No one ever saw him walking on earth again. He was gone, but his testimony remained. Genuine faith caused Enoch to walk so closely with God that he never experienced death. His life was a life of faith in the will of God.

God calls some to take a step of faith and do the highly unusual. It seems irrational. It invites criticism. This is often the nature of God's will. And unless God intervenes to let the world know that the project was actually His idea we can look like complete fools. Noah was such a man. God told Noah to build an ark in preparation for a great flood. I am sure Noah and his sons had no problem gathering the materials and building that big boat. The problem was that they began building it miles and miles from any major body of water. To make matters worse, Noah warned of a coming flood in an era when there was no such thing as rainfall. In that day only the dew watered the earth. Noah had to look like a complete idiot. Indeed he looked like a fool until the rain began to fall and the waters began to rush through the villages. God's Judgment had come. Noah was no fool for hearing God and doing His will. The foolish were those who refused to listen to the preacher of God's righteousness and do the will of God. Noah was a godly witness to a wicked generation. Every disciple of Jesus Christ ought to bear witness of Him to the lost (Acts 1:8). This is the will of God.

Other examples of faithful followers include Abraham, Sarah and the Patriarchs. They all had faith that God would fulfill His promises. Abraham heard from God to go to a land of promise that He would show him. By faith Abraham obeyed and set out to discover this land "not knowing where he was going"(Heb 11:8b). The will of God for Abraham was to begin a journey of faith and wait for God to lead him to "the city which has foundations, whose builder and maker is God"(Heb 11:10). Sarah too, alongside Abraham, had faith to conceive and give birth to a child when she was far too old "because she judged Him faithful who had promised" (11:12c). These all died clinging to a heavenly hope by faith: "These all died in faith, not having received the promises, but having seen them afar off were assured of them, embraced them and confessed that they were strangers and pilgrims on earth"(Hebrews 11:13).

By faith Isaac, the only son of Abraham, would be Divinely delivered from death atop Mount Moriah (vv.17-19) and bless his sons and each of the sons of Joseph who himself had by faith endured much affliction from his own family bur never stopped believing the promise of God to deliver His people from Egypt (Gen 50:24-26). He was so certain of God's promise that before his death he instructed the people to carry his remains back to Canaan when they left Egypt (Heb 11:20-21).

By faith Moses refused to be numbered with the worldly Egyptians and instead identified with the people of God and led them out of thraldom under Pharaoh (11:23-29). By faith Joshua succeeded Moses and led the people of God into the Promised Land having defeated all their enemies who stood in the way of the will of God (v.30).

One of the other notable persons of faith was a woman named Rahab. This girl is famous for much more than her faith. She was well known in her community for doing her deeds. The wrong kind! Rahab was a prostitute. Shameful was her way of life. Only a tool in the hands of men until the Lord transformed her. It is not fascinating that God would include the story of such an unclean individual among the role models of the Faith? Rahab was given opportunity to believe and serve the Lord and she seized the moment. She protected some spies by hiding them away in her home (see Joshua 2:1ff). Anyone can hear the call of God. Anyone can repent of sin. Anyone can trust and obey the will of God. Rahab the harlot did. You can too.

All of these godly people, and many others (Heb 11:32-40) were ordinary men and women with extraordinary faith. It is improbable that any of us will ever be famous for our faith like any one of them. Being famous is not the point. The point is to be faithful to God. Every saint of God should seek the Lord and have faith in Him to reveal His purpose and plan. So whatever the will for God may be for you, it will require faith and obedience. Are you ready for a wonderful and exciting journey of faith?

CHAPTER NINE

THE WILL OF GOD AND SUFFERING

"Therefore let those who suffer according to the will of God commit their souls to Him in doing good, as to a faithful creator." 1 Peter 4:19

Would God allow His children to suffer for doing His will? It may surprise many Christians to learn that the will of God often includes a degree of suffering. Believers can experience God's peace and joy in the midst of suffering, but it is no less suffering. This presents a problem. In fact, suffering has been a problem for myriads of people who wanted to believe that a good God would not allow bad things to happen to people who tried their best to be good. In our pursuit to discover the will of God we should keep in mind that God never promised a life of ease, comfort, and pleasure for those who follow Him. In fact, The Lord Jesus promised the exact opposite: "If anyone desires to come after me, let him deny himself, and take up his cross daily, and follow me" (Matthew 16:24). Pain and suffering is no real indication that Christians are out of the will of God. Ironically, it may be a good indication that they are doing exactly what He has called them to do.

The Problem of Suffering and God's Will

Where did suffering come from? How did it all begin? The trouble began in the Garden of Eden. God created Adam and Eve, the garden, and everything in it. It was all good! Adam and Eve had everything they needed. They lived in harmony with one another and with the animal kingdom. There was no conflict in the Garden until the old serpent (Satan) reared his head and began to question God's goodness (Gen 3:1-4). Eve got into a conversation with the devil, which is always a mistake. The serpent assured her that no negative consequence would come from eating the forbidden fruit, certainly not death (v.4b). In fact, he promised her that by ingesting the forbidden she would "be like God, knowing good and evil" (v.5). He lied. Eve took a bite, passed the fruit on to Adam and he ate it too. They disobeyed God and suffered the consequences of spiritual death and separation (Gen 3:7-24). In Adam, the human race fell (see Rom 5:12ff), and continues to suffer to this day. Suffering came when Man rebelled against God. Sin is the chief problem of all mankind, and every other problem we face is connected to it.

Concerning the Fall of man in the Garden of Eden, Billy Graham, in his wonderful book, *Hope for the Troubled Heart*, speaks clearly to the issue: "Man's direct disobedience resulted in the judgment of God placed on the human race. The beginning of all pain and suffering in the world started with one act of disobedience. Christian and non-Christian alike have inherited the consequences from our common ancestors, Adam and Eve – our polluted environment and flawed human nature."[16]

The consequences of original sin still plague the world today. Its curse will only be lifted as God's redemptive plan is completed at the end of the age when Christ comes back again. Many in the world today are not even aware of the true origin of suffering. Some may scoff even if they heard it. Believers, however, have a Christian world view. We understand that suffering and pain are in the world today because of what happened in Genesis chapter three. Pain was not in the plan of God for humankind. Pain and suffering came with sin. The beginning of physical suffering, the beginning of mental suffering, the beginning of spiritual suffering, the beginning of all suffering was due to the sin of man against Holy God.

No one born into this old sin-torn world will live a life free of pain and suffering. "He makes His sun rise on the evil and the good, and sends rain on the just and the unjust" (Matt 5:45b). The spiritual environment has been polluted by sin, and everyone within the global human network is under its curse. Christians too will have sorrow. In fact, Christians may be called to suffer even more than the unsaved. If you still find it hard to believe that God would require His children to endure suffering and pain, consider these passages from God's Word:

"For to you it has been granted on behalf of Christ, not only to believe in Him, but also to suffer for His sake."
- Philippians 1:29

"Yes, and all who desire to live godly in Christ Jesus will suffer persecution"
- 2 Timothy 3:12

"Many are the afflictions of the righteous, But the Lord delivers him out of them all."
- Psalm 34:19

Why does God allow it to happen to His children? We may never know all the reasons why God allows some suffering, but he Bible sheds light on some of His purposes.

The Purposes of Suffering in God's Will

God is good and He will only allow His children to suffer for some good purpose. Sometimes Christians suffer due to disobedience. We can not blame all of our suffering on God. Often, saints suffer due to bad choices they have made. Sin has consequences (Rom 3:23). God should never be blamed for causing suffering that is truly the result of personal sin.

Others suffer for no apparent reason. The suffering that God does allow in the lives of the righteous may be mysterious and puzzling in the minds of mortal men, but in God's Word I have discovered that God's people suffer for three basic reasons: (1) We suffer for the purpose of spiritual growth. (2) We suffer for the purpose of the gospel, and (3) we suffer for the purpose of God's glory.

The Growth Purpose

God's will is always sanctification (1 Thess 4:3-8). God expects us to keep on growing spiritually even through trial and tribulation. In fact, the Bible, in James 1:2, clearly teaches us that God uses suffering as a tool to shape us into the likeness of His Son: "My brethren, count it all joy when you fall into various trials, *knowing* that the testing of your faith produces patience. But let patience have its perfect work, that you may be perfect and complete, lacking nothing" (James 1:2).

Believers can rejoice through suffering because we know that God is using the trial to test our faith and make us stronger in the Lord. God uses trials and tribulations to shape us into the likeness of Christ. The growth purpose is vividly expressed in some verses that believers often recall when suffering. Paul said, "And we know that God causes all things to work together for *good* to those who love God, to those who are the called according to His purpose. For whom He foreknew, He also predestined to be conformed to the image of His Son, that He might be the firstborn among many brethren" (Romans 8:28-29). God is always working "good" and that good thing is that we are being shaped into the likeness of the Son of God. Jesus spoke of the branches of the vine needing pruning to produce good fruit (see John 15). God wants His children to be the very best so He prunes our lives to make us more and more fruitful for His kingdom work.

One way God uses people who have endured trial and suffering is to give them opportunity to help and comfort others who are suffering the same kinds of affliction: "Blessed be the God and Father of our Lord Jesus Christ, the Father of mercies and God of all comfort, who comforts us in all our tribulation, that we may be able to comfort those who are in any trouble, with the comfort with which we ourselves are comforted" (2 Corinthians 1:3-4).

The more we persevere and mature through our sufferings, the greater our usefulness in the hands of God.

The Gospel Purpose

Another reason the saints suffer is for the furtherance of the gospel of Jesus. We know that God desires for all people to be saved (1 Tim 2:4). God will sometimes allow suffering in the lives of His disciples for the purpose of leading lost souls to Christ. The apostle Paul was in prison when he wrote the letter to the saints at Philippi. They were concerned about his welfare, but he assured them that God was in control and that the suffering he endured was for the sake of the gospel:

> "But I want you to know, brethren, that the things which happened to me have actually turned out for the furtherance of the gospel, so that it has become evident to the whole palace guard, and to all the rest, that my chains are in Christ; and most of the

brethren in the Lord, having become confident by
my chains, are much more bold to speak the word
without fear."

- Philippians 1:12-14

Paul knew that he was in prison on purpose. All the palace guard
heard the gospel of Jesus Christ. In addition, other brethren waxed
bold in preaching the gospel because they knew Paul had been
imprisoned for it. Paul had to suffer persecution, but all heard the
gospel and he rejoiced because he could see that God had actually
allowed his imprisonment for more people to hear the good news
and believe. In fact, Jesus Himself came to earth on a gospel mission.
Was it the Father's will for Him to suffer and die? Absolutely. God
sent His Son to earth to live and to die that whoever believed in Him
would be saved (see Jn 3:16).

Brother Clyde

As a young man I remember the story of a man in our church named
Clyde. He became sick on one occasion and had to be hospitalized
for several days. He was placed in a room with another man that
he did not know. The days in the hospital gave brother Clyde the
opportunity to get to know this man and share the gospel with him.
He led him to Christ. Clyde came home from the hospital without
ever knowing why he was ill. He testified that he believed that God
had allowed the sickness to get him in the hospital to witness to that
man and lead him to Christ. I believe him. To God be the glory!

The Glory Purpose

Everything that God does in our lives is for His own glory. Peter
states clearly that suffering in the will of God is no reason to be
ashamed but to glorify God instead: "Yet if anyone suffers as a

Christian, let him not be ashamed, but let him glorify God in this matter" (1 Peter 4:16). It brings God glory to prepare His children for glory. God requires His children to suffer to some degree in preparation for being glorified with Him. The testing of our faith also prepares us for glory: "In this you greatly rejoice, though now for a little while, if need be, you have been grieved by various trials, that the genuineness of your faith, being much more precious than gold that perishes, though it be tested by fire, *may be found to praise, honor, and glory at the revelation of Jesus Christ"* (1 Peter 1:6-7).

Jesus suffered and died on the cross before being exalted to the Father's right hand where He reigns above all authorities, whether angelic or demonic (see 1 Peter 3:18-22). If Jesus was required to suffer before being exalted again to glory then the same is required of His followers.

God even allows some to suffer in unusual ways that His glory may be displayed in them. Jesus and His disciples came to a man blind from birth and the disciples thought his blindness was the result of his sin or his parents sin (see John 9:1-2). When the disciples asked Jesus "who sinned," He gave them a surprising answer: "Neither this man nor his parents sinned, but that the *works of God should be revealed in him"* (John 9:3). God allowed this man to suffer with his blind condition from birth so that Jesus would come and heal him to the glory of God. As a result, the blind man was healed and believed in Jesus. His life became a glowing example of the saving power of the Son of God.

The Privilege of Suffering in God's Will

It is a privilege indeed to suffer for doing what is right. If we suffer for the cause of Christ and point others to Him, that kind of suffering turns out to be a good thing. Peter contends, "For it is better, if it is the will of God, to *suffer for doing good* than for doing evil" (1 Peter 3:17).

The Bible says we suffer in the will of God and out of the will of God. In other words, much of our suffering is due to poor choices. Many Christians suffer heartache, and sometimes physically because they chose to disobey the truth of God's Word. So before we go any further, we need to examine our hearts and lives to see if we are sinning against God. Am I suffering due to some act of disobedience? We must be certain that we have that "good conscience" (1 Pet 3:16) and that we are nor suffering due to our own acts of rebellion against God. It is no privilege to suffer for wrongdoing. And it is a disgrace to God for any believer to rebel against Him, suffer the consequences of personal sin, and then claim to "suffer for Jesus sake." Much of the suffering in the church today is not due to doing "right" but doing "wrong." Peter asked, "what good is it if you do what is wrong and suffer for that?(1 Pet 2:20). The answer: It does no good! Suffering is only "good" if it is in the will of God.

If our suffering is due to obeying God, we should count it a privilege to suffer for His name. Suffering in the will of God means God is using our lives to impact others for His kingdom and to bring glory to Himself. Paul told the Philippians they were not only called to believe in Christ for salvation but also to "suffer for His sake" (Phil 1:29). In the Great Commission work of the early church, the apostles were beaten for preaching the gospel, and went away rejoicing that they had been chosen to suffer for His name (Acts 5:40-42). And let us not forget that Jesus "also suffered" in the will of God for the purpose of saving our souls to the glory of God (1 Peter 3:18). Jesus lived his years on earth in obedience to the Father's will and for His glory! When we must suffer in the will of God, let's count it a privilege and persevere until the end.

The call to suffer and sacrifice should be no real surprise to those of us who know freedom in the United States of America. Many of our military veterans in years past, have gladly gone into some foreign and hostile territory and risked their own lives to fight for our country and for the sake of freedom. They considered it an honor to serve. It is an honor to serve the King of kings who greatly suffered for us, even if our suffering is a necessary part of accomplishing His will. Jesus had this attitude toward suffering, even the shameful death on the cross (Phil 2:5-11). What a privilege to suffer in the name of our Lord Jesus Christ who suffered and died for us!

The Principles of Suffering in God's Will (1 Peter 4:12-19)

Peter's first epistle was written to saints who were suffering persecution. The apostle wrote to encourage those believers to persevere in the Faith and laid down eight principles for them, and us, to live by. When Believers suffer persecution, they should respond with confidence that God is in control and that He is working all things together for good (Rom 8:28-29).

Do not be Surprised (v.12)

One fellow joined the Army to gain all the "benefits" of serving in the United States military. Conflict started in the Middle East, and he was told he was being deployed to the war zone. He said, "You mean me?" "Nobody told me when I joined the army that we would be in a war." Did anyone tell you when you became a Christian that you would be in a spiritual war? Now that you are in the Lord's army, do not be surprised about the conflict. The world, the flesh, and the devil will be out to get you. Believers should not think that some unusual or "strange" thing is happening to them (v.12b).

Jesus also said, "Do not marvel that the world hates you, they hated me first" (Jn 15:18). John passed along the same truth (1 Jn 3:13). In addition, we should not be surprised about suffering because we have learned that God will allow some trial and tribulation in our lives for the purpose of refining our faith and shaping us into the likeness of Christ. The "fiery trial" (1 Peter 4:12a) not only portrays a painful experience of persecution, but it was also used to describe a furnace melting down metal to purge it of its impurities (see 1:6-7). God desires our faith to grow, so expect Him to use trial and tribulation to test our faith. Suffering is real. Christ Himself suffered in the will of the Father, so will we to some degree.

Joyfully participate in the Sufferings of Christ (v.13)

Our suffering is spiritually connected to the sufferings of Jesus. Peter says, "Christ also suffered" (1 Peter 3:18). It seems so strange to consider that we could actually rejoice in the midst of trial and tribulation, but that is what the Bible teaches us. The apostles, who had been arrested, imprisoned, and then beaten for preaching the gospel of Jesus Christ, went away rejoicing that they were considered worthy to suffer for His name (see Acts 5:29-42). Paul also stated that he shared in the sufferings of Christ with the assurance that God was preparing him for the day when he would be called home to heaven and be glorified (see Phil 3:10-14). Christians rejoice in His sufferings because of the assurance that they will soon share in His glory with great joy at the consummation of the age. Each day, even in the midst of suffering, believers anticipate the Second Coming when our joy will be made full in His eternal presence.

Look Forward to your Reward in Heaven (v.13b)

There will be joy in the presence of God for His children and great reward. God will reward those who suffer in His will. We should not focus on how bad we have it now, but we should look forward to how wonderful it will be in heaven where we will be rewarded for suffering for the cause of Christ. "To the extent" indicates that a believer's reward in heaven will be proportionate to their earthly suffering. "At the revelation of His glory" (v.13b) refers to Christ's return. When Jesus comes back again at the consummation of the age all suffering will cease and the godly will be rewarded for persevering under trial. Jesus also spoke of reward in heaven for those who suffer for Him on earth: "Blessed are you when men hate you, and when they exclude you, and revile you, and cast out your name as evil, for the Son of Man's sake. Rejoice in that day and leap for joy! *For indeed your reward is great in heaven,* for in like manner their fathers did to the prophets" (Luke 6:22-23).

Count insults as Blessings through the Power of the Spirit (v.14)

The Spirit of glory rests upon you and me if we are "reproached" for the name of Christ (v.14). God blesses believers who are insulted for serving Jesus. He blesses them with a special presence of His Holy Spirit to help them endure the suffering and to accomplish His will on earth. Therefore, we can count the insults as blessings. Every time you are insulted for living for Jesus, God turns those insults into blessings!

Do not be Ashamed but glorify God (v.16)

When we suffer because of our own sinfulness we should be ashamed, but when we suffer for doing right we should not be ashamed but give glory to God in the suffering. The way some of these televangelist talk, many of God's people are feeling guilty about being in a financial struggle, sick and suffering. People are often told, "It's your fault because you do not have enough faith." Ironically, the suffering actually is an indication of a solid and growing faith. God is working in the lives of His children to bring them to maturity. He will deal with the ungodly on the Day of Judgment.

Trust God to deal with the Ungodly (17-18)

If a saint sins against you, God will deal with him through correction. If a sinner sins against you God will deal with him through condemnation. Saints suffer now at the hands of their persecutors, but the ungodly will suffer for eternity, unless they repent and believe in Jesus. We can trust God to deal with our persecutors. Vengeance belongs to the Lord (Rom 10:19).

Entrust your soul to God (19a)

Just as we trust God to recompense others who sin against us, so we must also commit our souls to Him. To commit our souls to God is to place our lives into His hands completely. To "commit" is to "entrust." It is a banker's term referring to a deposit for safe keeping. Jesus used the same word on the cross when He committed His spirit to the Father (see Luke 23:46). In the midst of suffering we must entrust our entire beings to God's sovereign control. He is the "Faithful creator." He is good and powerful at the same time. He can handle whatever comes, and He will be faithful and enable us to persevere until the end (1 Cor 10:13).

Shadrach, Meshach, and Abed-Nego proved to be excellent examples of entrusting everything to God. They would not bow and worship before the king's idol even in the face of the furnace of fire. They trusted God and He delivered them (see Dan 3:1-25). We can trust the Lord to do what is best for us and to empower us to do "good."

Do the right thing (19b)

Suffering in the will of God can drive us away from God, or it can draw us closer to Him. Doing the right thing is not always easy. Suffering at the hand of another may lead to anger, bitterness, and an unforgiving spirit. Forgiving others is the right thing to do. Having been crucified, Jesus prayed to God, "Father forgive them for they know not what they do" (Luke 23:34).

How can we do the right thing? Does God really expect His children to respond in a Christ-like fashion in the midst of persecution? Yes. But none of us can do it without His help. Actually, it is God's will that we "silence" our persecutors by doing what is "good" (1 Pet 2:15). And it takes the power of the Holy Spirit to do what is "good." Only through the grace and strength of the Lord can we "do the right thing." The "Spirit of glory," or the power of the Holy Spirit is already in us and upon us (1 Pet 4:14b). It is this wonderful truth of God's power to accomplish His will that we will explore next.

CHAPTER TEN

GOD'S POWER AND GOD'S WILL

"He who calls you is faithful, who will also do it"1 Thessalonians 5:24

When I was in fourth grade I had a girlfriend. Actually, several of my friends in our class also considered "Annie" to be their girlfriend too. I thought if I could impress her, she would be *all mine*! One day at recess, with the girl watching, I climbed up high atop the backstop fence on the playground ball field. As I was about half-way to the top of that fence, about 10 feet up, I heard a teacher call my name. I now refer to her as "Mrs. Grouch." I remember her exact words: "Micah Lane, I hope you fall." Needless to say, I fell. I remember feeling the chain links brushing my fingertips as I made my decent. I hit hard. The right ankle sprained terribly. I tried to stand on my own, but just sat back down in pain and lots of tears. (I am sure the girl was impressed!). I thought I had broken my ankle. And I never wanted to see that teacher again. It was the worse day of my childhood.

Then there was my friend, Patrick Thompson.

He did sweat. But he was the only one willing to help me. He picked me up off the sandy ground and placed my arm around his neck. As I stood, on the good leg, he said, "Micah, I will get you back to the classroom. Just hold on and lean on me as we go." I did. Wherever Patrick went so did I. When he went left, I went left. When he went to the right, I did too. He walked with me all the way back to the classroom and sat me down at my desk. The entire journey, I just leaned on Patrick. It was his strength that carried us. I just walked along beside him in complete dependence. Here is the key to success in the will of God. It is not us, but Christ (Gal 2:20). We must learn to lean on Him.

The secret to success is the power of the Spirit that is unleashed in the lives of believers as they submit to the Lordship of Christ. Jesus empowers us by His Holy Spirit to live for Him, serve, and to fulfill the Great Commission to the glory of God (Acts 1:8). Believers are enabled to walk in God's will by His "grace" (2 Tim 2:1). He calls us to do His will, and then He faithfully does it Himself as we depend on Him (1 Thess 5:24). God does not expect us to accomplish His will in our own strength.

Jesus walked, taught, preached, and carried out His ministry on earth in the power of the Holy Spirit. Even the demons had to flee when Jesus spoke to them with authority (Matt 12:25-28; Mark 1:21-28: 5:1-20). John baptized Jesus in the Jordan River, and upon coming up out of the water, the Holy Spirit, like a dove, descended upon Him (Matt 3:16). Jesus then began his ministry being "led by the Spirit" into the desert places to be tempted by the devil (Matt 4:1-11). The implication being the Son did the will of His Father in the power of the Spirit.

Jesus taught His disciples to depend completely on the Holy Spirit as they implemented the global task of the Great Commission (Acts 1:1-8). The apostles went preaching, performing miracles, and casting out demons in the name of Jesus Christ and by the power of the Holy Spirit (see Acts 2:1-39, 43; 3:1-10, 4:1-4, 5-12, 32-37; 5:12-16; 6:8-15; 7:54-60; 8:4-8, 9-25, 26-40; 9:20-43; 34-48; 16:16-24, 25-34). They were mere men and attributed all the glory to Christ who worked the miracles and wonders through them (Acts 10:24-26; 14:11-18).

Paul concisely stated the secret to Christian living and fruitful ministry that he learned as he did the will of God: "I know how to be abased, and I know how to abound. Everywhere and in all things I have learned both to be in full and to be hungry, both to abound and suffer need. I can do all things through Christ who strengthens me" (Philippians 4:12-13). Paul said he had *learned* the secret to Christian living. What is the secret? The secret to doing the will of God is that God does it through us by the power of the Holy Spirit. He had learned to deny himself and live by faith in the Jesus (Gal 2:20). All Christians must learn to lean on Christ. Saints must depend on the Spirit. Paul did not say he could do all things in his own strength personally. He boldly confessed that the power to please God and to accomplish His work on earth is found only in a personal relationship with Jesus Christ. In His strength we can do all things. Apart from Him we can do nothing (John 15:5). Have you learned the secret of living and ministering in the power of the Holy Spirit?

A Promised Helper

In the Old Testament, through the prophet Joel, God made a promise that a blessed day would come when the Spirit of God would indwell all of His children (see Joel 2). The Lord Jesus also promised His disciples that the Spirit would come to indwell them and to help them after His ascension:

> "And I will pray the Father, and He will give you another Helper, that He may abide with you forever, even the Spirit of truth, whom the world cannot receive, because it neither sees Him nor knows Him;

> but you know Him, for He dwells with you and will
> be in you."
>
> - John 14:16-17

> "Nevertheless I tell you the truth. It is to your
> advantage that I go away; for if I do not go away,
> the Helper will not come to you; but if I depart, I
> will send Him to you."
>
> - John 16:7

Jesus knew that the Disciples could not possibly succeed in doing the will of God on earth without Divine assistance. Therefore, God promised to send the Spirit to help them. The challenge of living and speaking for God and doing His will is far too demanding for any person without help from heaven.

A promise for help is no help at all unless that promise is kept. Has a friend ever promised to help you? Did that friend keep the promise? Friends sometimes fail to keep the promises they have made. Broken promises cause one to wonder if they have a friend they can count on. Is anyone truly faithful? Jesus certainly is! God the Father is faithful to keep all of His promises. Jesus came and taught His disciples that the Promise of the Father, the Holy Spirit, would come "not many days" after He was taken up into heaven to sit at God's right hand (Acts 1:5b). And, of course, the Spirit came to indwell the disciples just as Jesus said He would.

A Present Helper

The promise the God the Father made to send the Holy Spirit to indwell His children was fulfilled on the day of Pentecost (see Acts 2:1-4). The Holy Spirt comes into a person's life the moment they place their faith in Christ as their Lord and Savior (Eph 1:13-14). Any person that does not have the Holy Spirit is not saved (Rom 8:9).

But did Jesus not tell the disciples to wait in Jerusalem until they received power from heaven? Yes indeed. Jesus told His disciples to tarry in Jerusalem until the Spirit came from heaven with power (see Luke 24:49; Acts 1:4). They waited in prayer in the upper room until the Spirit came upon them from heaven like a mighty rushing wind and filled the place where they were assembled (Acts 2:2). In his sermon on this special Day of Pentecost, Peter acknowledged that this divine event was the promised Holy Spirit, whom God sent to indwell the believers upon the exaltation of His Son, Jesus Christ, to the highest place (Acts 2:14-36). Therefore, The Spirit now indwells all those who believe. There is no more waiting on the Holy Spirit to come. He is here. The Holy Spirit is in your life if you are a believer in Jesus Christ. Often we do not "feel" the Spirit so we are tempted to think that He is not present. But He is with us whether we "feel" His presence or not.

In our Texas home, we had a skunk that would frequently come by our house. In fact, on certain nights he walked under the house. That skunk had a way of making his presence known. He would come and go. We always knew when he was visiting. Thank God he did not take up housekeeping! The Holy Spirit is within the heart of every Christian. He does not come and go. He is in your heart until He takes you home to heaven or until Jesus comes back again to earth. We should never wonder if the Spirit is with us, nor wait to see if He will manifest Himself to us. We should claim the presence of the Holy Spirit in our lives each day as we endeavor to discover and do the will of God. By the Spirit, Jesus is with us always, even to the end of the age (see Matt 28:20). The Great commission is a great responsibility but we need not fear, God is always with us. He will never leave us nor forsake us (Heb 13:5).

A Personal Helper

The Holy Spirit is a personal being. He is the Spirit of Christ in us. He is not merely an influence or thing. He is a person. Jesus referred to the Holy Spirit as another "helper," one just like Him (John 14:16). The compound word in Greek is *paracletos*.[17] This word speaks of one who comes along side to help. Jesus lives within our lives through the presence of the Spirit. In fact, the Holy Spirit is Christ in us. Jesus said, "I will not leave you as orphans, I will come to you" (John 14:18).

Christ maintains the personal relationship we have with Him by living within our hearts. The Spirit convicts of sin and guides believers into the truth (see John 16:8-14). The Spirit also helps God's children pray as they should, even when we do not know how. The Spirit "makes intercession for the saints according to the will of God" (Rom 8:26-27). He reproduces the "fruit" of Christ-like character (Gal 5:22-23). If a person does not have an intimate walk with God, it is not God's fault. He personally resides in the heart of every believer to shape us into the likeness of Jesus (Rom 8:29). God keeps it personal because He is a personal God. He not only wants to do great works through us, He wants to draw us closer to Him. He wants us to walk in fellowship with Him. He wants us to know Him.

Our sons are Star Wars fans. They learned the phase: "May the force be with you." It sounds so impersonal to me. God does not work in the lives of His children in a detached fashion. He is personal. Our helper from heaven is not a "thing" but a person. The Christian's strength is found in a personal relationship with Christ. Our helper is not some impersonal force, but a close and personal friend who communicates with us, encourages us, assures us, and empowers us to do the will of God.

A Powerful Helper

The Holy Spirit is God. The power of the Spirit unleashed in the lives of believers enables them to live in holiness (1 Thess 5:23), bear the fruit of the Spirit (Gal 5:22-23), proclaim the gospel to a lost world (Acts 1:8), and do whatever is in the will of God (Phil 4:13). Think about it. God's power is at work in you and through you to accomplish His will. How can you fail?

The Holy Spirit was active in the creation (Gen1:2). Jesus carried out His ministry on earth of teaching, healing, and casting out demons by the power of the Spirit (Matt 12:28). It was the power of the Holy Spirit that raised Jesus Christ from the grave on that first Easter Sunday (Eph 1:19-20). If The power of the Spirt accomplished all of these miraculous acts of God, then we can be certain that He can handle any situation we will ever face. Jesus said that once He was exalted on high to His Father's right hand, His followers would then do even greater works than He through the power of the Spirit: "Most assuredly, I say to you, he who believes in Me, the works that I dohe will do also; and *greater works* than these he will do, because I go to My Father" (John 14:12). We do "good works" for God by the power of the Holy Spirit (see Matt 5:16). There is no power greater than the power of God. In our own strength we are certain to fall short; but in the power of the Lord Jesus Christ, we are more than conquerors (Rom 8:37).

Why then do believers seem to be so powerless? If God indwells His children by His Spirit to empower them to live and work for Him, why then is the church so spiritually weak? Why do so many born again disciples of Jesus Christ feel like failures in their pursuit of the will of God? What is missing in the local church?

Filling of the Spirit

The answer to the believer's dilemma of powerlessness is the fullness of the Holy Spirit. By faith, the saints can be filled with divine power

(Micah 3:8). God gave us His Holy Spirit to empower us for the purpose of fulfilling the Great Commission (Acts 1:8). All of God's children have the Holy Spirit indwelling, but not all are under His continual influence. To possess the Spirit is not the same as living under His control. It is an issue of Lordship and surrender. Paul gave the command for the saints to let the indwelling Holy Spirit take control:

> "And do not be drunk with wine, which is dissipation; but be filled with the Spirit, speaking to one another in psalms and hymns and spiritual songs, singing and making melody in your heart to the Lord, giving thanks always for all things to God the Father in the name of our Lord Jesus Christ, submitting to one another in the fear of God."
> -Ephesians 5:18-21

The command "be filled with the Spirit" calls for all believers to be continually "controlled and impelled" by the Holy Spirit.[18] If a person is drunk they are under the influence of the alcohol. Their behavior is changed in a most negative fashion. In contrast, the Spirit fills and changes believers in a positive and godly way, blessing their hearts with joy, gratitude, and mutual respect (Eph 5:19-21). The Holy Spirit takes over and reproduces the Divine qualities of Christ-like character (Gal 5:22-23). With the filling of the Spirit disciples are empowered to fulfill the Great Commission (Acts 1:8). Without the fullness of the Spirit, it is impossible to discover and do the will of God to the glory of God. John MacArthur concurs: "No Christian can fulfill God's will for his life apart from being filled with His Spirit. If we do not obey this command, we cannot obey any other – simply because we cannot do any of God's will apart from God's Spirit."[19]

The filling of the Spirit is also a repeated experience.[20] The Holy Spirit would maintain His impelling influence in the hearts of the children of God moment by moment, twenty-four seven. Nothing stands in the way of believers continually being filled with the Spirit and experiencing His supernatural power in the will of God with the exception of sin. Disobedience quenches the Spirit (1 Thess 5:19). Confession and repentance cleanses the heart and makes everything right with the Lord (1 John 1:9).

Lights on?

If you walk over to the light switch in the living room and turn the light off, you are in the dark. Does that mean you have had a power failure? Is your home without power? Of course not. You have plenty of power. The problem is that the flow of the power stopped when you turned the switch off. The problem we have in the church is not a lack of power. The problem is a stoppage of the *flow* of power. The power of God's Spirit is present in the lives of believers but often the evidence of that Divine power is almost nonexistent. Others rarely "see Jesus" in the lives of many Christians because they have some unconfessed sin in their lives and the "light" of the Lord is not shining through them like it should (Matt 5:14-16). Sin is the problem. God's people have to realize the error of their way and repent. Otherwise, discovering and doing the will of God is out of the question.

If you are willing to completely surrender to the Lordship of Jesus Christ, the Holy Spirit will empower you in that moment to do the will of the Father. He loves you unconditionally. Jesus died on the cross, paid the penalty for our sins, and rose from the grave on the third day giving us victory. The Holy Spirit has also gifted every follower of Christ with some special endowments that fit perfectly into the plan of God. Discovering these gifts of the Holy Spirit can be a tremendous help in the discovery God's will. It is this wonderful possibility that we will explore in the next chapter.

CHAPTER ELEVEN

THE WILL OF GOD AND SPIRITUAL GIFTS

"As each one has received a gift, minister it to one another, as good stewards of the manifold grace of God."1 Peter 4:10-11

When I graduated from Southwestern Baptist Theological Seminary, my father and my step-mother gave me gifts. As I unwrapped the weighty package I immediately realized that the gifts inside were connected to my calling. They gave me a set of commentaries on the New Testament by Warren Wiersbe. It was a gift suitable to a young pastor. Very practical. I could use these "tools" to prepare expository sermons from God's Word and fulfill my calling in the local church. Father knew what I needed. He gave the perfect gift.

The gifts of God are always suitable for accomplishing His purposes to His glory. He knows exactly what we need. Our gifts from the Holy Spirit are directly connected to the will of God for our lives. God the Father gives His children gifts to use in service to Him. Gifts are tools to be used in service to others. A high school principal or administrator may be given the gift of administrations (1 Cor 12:28). A president would need the gift of leadership (Rom

12:8a). A nurse may have the gift of mercy (Rom 12:8b). Pastors and teachers, of course, need the gift of teaching (Eph 4:11; 1 Cor 12:29; 1 Peter 4:11). Whatever God calls a person to accomplish in life is undergirded by the talents and gifts of His grace.

When you discover your spiritual gifts then you have discovered much of God's will for your life. God will position you to exercise your gifts of the Holy Spirit to help others and bring glory to Himself. Saints who discover their spiritual gifts will be able to narrow their focus on a particular area of ministry. God would never endow His children with gifts or talents that He did not expect them to use to bring Him glory (Matt 25:14-30; 1 Peter 4:10-11). To know our Spiritual gifts is to know the kind of work in which God desires for us to engage. Once I was certain that God had called me and gifted me to be a pastor-teacher it was apparent that I should begin praying for an open door of ministry in a local church (Col 4:2-4). God had it all planned before I was saved (Eph 2:10). It has been a wonderful journey of discovery and blessing as I have seen the hand of God positioning me to fulfill His will with the gifts that He has so graciously given.

Gifted *with* the Spirit at Salvation

The Holy Spirit Himself is a "gift" from Heaven (Acts 2:38). He personally comes into a person's life the moment they repent of sin and place their faith in Christ as their Lord and Savior (Eph 1:13-14). The person and presence of the Spirit is a gift from God in the lives of *all* of His children. He assures believers in their hearts that they belong to God (Rom 8:16). The Holy Spirit is a heavenly mark of divine ownership in every Christian's life and the guarantee of eternal life (2 Cor 1:21-22). Any person who does not have the Holy Spirit indwelling is not saved. Paul says, "But you are not in the flesh but in the Spirit, if indeed the Spirit of God dwells in you. Now if anyone does not have the Spirit of Christ, he is not His" (Romans

8:9). The Holy Spirit is the gift of God who assigns a variety of spiritual gifts to the children of God.

Gifted *by* the Spirit

When the Holy Spirit comes to indwell a new believer, He brings some very special and Spiritual gifts with Him (1 Cor 12:11). Like a newborn baby who receives gifts at birth, so a person who experiences the new birth receives at least one gift from the Holy Spirit at their conversion.[21] A new born child may not understand what gift or even that he has received a gift, but a gift has been given. Many new Christians may not be aware that they have already received a gift from the Holy Spirit, but they are gifted none the less.

The word "gift"refers to spiritual gifts (1 Peter 4:10a). The apostle Paul also used the same term to refer to gifts from the Holy Spirit (Rom 12:6; 1 Cor 1:7; 12:4,9,28, 30-31; 1 Tim 1:6). The Spirit chooses a gift and gives it to a believer for service (1 Cor 12:7). Saints need not go shopping for any spiritual gifts. God the Holy Spirit has already chosen the gifts and He distributes them "to each one individually as He wills" (1 Cor 12:11b).

There are five passages in the New Testament where many of the gifts of the Holy Spirit are listed (see Rom 12:3-8; 1 Cor 12:8-10; 12:28-30; Eph 4:11; 1 Peter 4:9-11). All believers are gifted according to the "manifold grace of God" (1 Pet 4:10c). The word "manifold" literally means "multicolored" or "many faceted."[22] God's grace manifests itself in various ways. It has many different aspects. The gifts are richly varied. The gifts you have been given are perfectly suited for you and what God has called you to do. The way God uses it in your life is unique to you and your good work of ministry. No one can do what you do the same way you do it to the glory of God. You, your gifts, and your ministry are special in the eyes of God. Because God has been so gracious in His gift giving to His children, we should be "good stewards" and use the gifts we have received (1 Peter 4:10b).

Gifted to Serve

Peter says that Christians should "minister" their gifts "to one another" (1 Peter 4:10). "Minister" is a word that means to serve others in a variety of ways.[23] It is the same root from which we get the word deacon. The gifts that God the Holy Spirit has given are to be exercised, employed, worked, or used. A gift that is unused is a waste. God does not want His children wasting the time, talents, opportunities, or gifts that He has given them by His grace. To faithfully serve others via the gifts we have received is to be a "good steward" (1 Peter 4:10b). A steward is the same as a "manager" or a trustee.[24] The word was often used to speak of a responsible slave. We have been entrusted with these gifts from God. We are responsible to put them to work helping others for His glory. To give God the glory we must (1) acknowledge, (2) appreciate, (3) ascertain and (4) apply our spiritual gifts as we serve others in the power of the Holy Spirit.

1. Believers should acknowledge their spiritual gifts.

The first step to serving God with our Spiritual gifts is to accept the fact that we are gifted. "As each has received a gift" (v.10) is a clear indication that all of the believers to whom Peter was writing had received a gift. They did not need to ask for a gift. They needed to realize that they had been given a gift and use it to serve others to the glory of God. Many will never serve the Lord until they acknowledge that He has endowed them with natural talents, abilities, and a special gift from the Holy Spirit. Too many followers of Christ excuse themselves from any ministry activity because they have been deceived into thinking that they possess no ability, talent, or gift. But no child of God is neglected. Each born again believer has (past tense) already received at least one gift of the Holy Spirit. We should claim the truth of the Word by faith and thank God that we are able to serve Him.

2. Believers should appreciate their spiritual gifts.

I think it is essential that we thank God for the gift or gifts that He has given to us. It is the will of God that the saints always give thanks to Him in every circumstance (1 Thess 5:18). We should begin our quest of serving God by being thankful to the giver of gifts, even if we do not fully understand what gift or gifts we have received from the Holy Spirit Godly parents usually desire only one thing from their children in return for gifts– thanksgiving. The least we can do for the one giving a gift is to thank them for their generosity. God is pleased that His children gives thanks to Him for the gifts that He bestows by His grace. God the Father must be grieved over ungrateful children who are discontent and unhappy with the gifts He has chosen for them. Some believers do not appreciate the gifts they have received. They prefer a different gift. Some would like to return the gift and pick out one they like better. Have you ever taken a gift back to the Mall for exchange? We often return items to the retailer to exchange worldly goods. But a gift from the Spirit is a heavenly blessing. God has gifted His children with purpose.

It seems many are not content with the gifts that God has chosen for them. Why are people often unhappy with the gifts God has given them? Every gift is important in the work of the Kingdom. Each gift can and should be used to minister to the saints to the glory of God. Peter divided the gifts into two categories – Speaking gifts and Serving gifts (I would add another category from Paul, "Sign gifts"- miracles, healings, and tongues) and Peter treats each category and each gift equally under God. The Bible never says that one gift makes a person more valuable than another.

Often believers evaluate their gifts from the world's perspective and desire what might be called the more "flashy" gifts. The carnally minded like to be gifted so they may receive attention and recognition. And if praises and accolades are not plentiful, self decides to shop around for gifts better suited to the ego. But the gifts chosen by the Spirit for us are the ones that bring God glory. It is all about Jesus, never about us. Spiritual gifts are not given to make us feel better, but to serve others. Let us be thankful and serve to the glory of God!

3. Believers should apply their spiritual gifts.

"Spiritual Gifts are to be used to the glory of God and the building up of the church."[25] Gifts are not worth possessing if they are not used. When you received a gift for Christmas did you use it? Have you worn that shirt or does it just hang in the closet? What about that new book you were given? Are you reading it? Gifts are only beneficial if they are used. Each Christmas we receive gift cards to restaurants in the Myrtle Beach area, and we use them! Our church family likes for us to eat well. If we did not put those gift cards to use, they would never accomplish their intended purpose. Spiritual gifts are not for storage. The gifts of the Holy Spirit should always be exercised for the edification of the Body of Christ and for His glory (1 Peter 4:10-11).

4. Believers should ascertain (discover) their spiritual gifts.

How do we discover the gift(s) that God has given us? Discovering Spiritual gifts may not be as complex as some make it out to be. Many Christians come to know their gifts from the Spirit as they mature in their walk with the Lord. As the days, weeks, months, and even years pass in the life of a Christian, one may come to understand that God has gifted them in many ways. God reveals them in His own time. Some gifts are discovered only after a person begins serving in a ministry or missions opportunity.

I encourage new believers to do three basic things to help them discover their gifts from the Holy Spirit: (1) Surrender, (2) seek the Lord, and (3) serve the Lord in any way they can.

Gift discovery begins with complete surrender to God (Rom 12:1-2). The believer in Jesus who is totally committed to Him will seek the Lord until he discovers the gifts of the Spirit that have been bestowed upon him. Billy Graham concurs: "I believe a person who is Spirit-filled – constantly submitting to the Lordship of Christ– will come to discover his gifts with some degree of ease. He wants God to guide in his life, and that is the kind of person God stands ready to bless by showing him the gifts the Holy Spirit has bestowed upon him."[26]

The fully surrendered person will stay in touch with God through prayer and meditation on the Word until God makes it clear how He has gifted them. The committed Christian will also begin serving the Lord at the first opportunity. Pray for an opportunity (see Col 4:2). God will open a door for you to serve Him in some ministry today. Do not wait until you know all of your gifts before you get involved in the work of the Lord. Some gifts you will only discover as you begin to exercise them. It may be another brother or sister in the Lord who comes to you and tells you how they can see God at work in your life as you serve others.

Your vital part in the Great Commission should not wait until you have discovered and developed all of your Spiritual gifts. The task is urgent and all believers should get involved immediately. It is the urgency of the Great Commission of our Lord Jesus Christ that we will come to grips with in our next chapter.

FOR FURTHER STUDY

Criswell, W. A. *The Baptism, Filling, & Gifts of the Holy Spirit.* Grand Rapids: Zondervan, 1973.

Graham, Billy. *The Holy Spirit.* Dallas: Word Publishing, 1988.

Hemphill, Ken. *You are Gifted.* Nashville: Broadman & Holman, 2009.

Ibid., *Serving God: Discovering & Using your Spiritual Gifts Workbook.* Nashville: The Sampson Company, 1995.

McRae, William. *Dynamics of Spiritual Gifts.* Grand Rapids: Zondervan, 1976.

Packer, J. I. *Keep In Step with the Spirit.* Grand Rapids: Baker Books, 2005.

Stanley, Charles. *The Wonderful Spirit Filled Life.* Nashville: Thomas Nelson, 1992.

Vines, Jerry. *Spirit Life.* Nashville: Broadman & Holman Publishers, 1998.

Wagner, C. Peter. *Discover Your Spiritual Gifts.* Ventura, California: Regal Books, 2012.

CHAPTER TWELVE

THE GREAT COMMISSION: GOD'S WILL FOR THE LOCAL CHURCH

"But you shall receive power when the Holy Spirit has come upon you; and you shall be witnesses to Me in Jerusalem, and in all Judea, and Samaria, and to the end of the earth." Acts 1:8

The family van broke down again. Surprised? I certainly wasn't. After 220,000 miles, repairs were needed frequently and getting more and more expensive. We decided to donate the old "ministry mobile" to charity. The idea of giving it away left us with a good feeling but the need for another vehicle remained.

Being a one car family does not work well for ministers. We thought we could endure for a while with only one, but we knew we would soon have to acquire another automobile. But how? You know our dilemma. The money just was not in the account. With all of our financial responsibilities and a son in college, we simply could not afford another sizable monthly payment. It would be more than we would be able to manage without getting into a financial bind. I was certain God had promised me an "inheritance," which

I understood to be assurance that He would meet our need, but the day had arrived and I had no means of transportation for ministry. What would I do? Where would the money come from? How?

God is the God of "how."

Each year in our wonderful church, God's people have what is called "Pastor Appreciation Sunday." This is one of my favorite days of the year! You know the routine. A love offering is received for the pastor and his family. All the saints give extra to make the pastor feel extra special. Be sure that your church has a special day to honor the hardworking pastor (1Tim 5:17-18). All of God's under-shepherds need lots of encouragement, respect, honor, and love. The extra money helps too. Give as much as you can.

The "Big Sunday" for the pastor was still over a month away. Each day we prayed for God's guidance and the new automobile. We decided to use the upcoming love offering as a down payment toward a car. We prayed for the amount of the offering to match the need for the vehicle that God would like for us to have. We had no idea what God would do. And what He did was miraculous (see Eph 3:20-21).

Before we gave the van away we decided to have it repaired one more time. A friend at church recommended a local mechanic. The estimate sounded fair, so I asked him to see if he could get the old "ministry mobile" on the road again. It took him a couple of days, but he succeeded. When the mechanic had finished his work, he called to tell me everything looked good with one minor problem. The front tire on the passenger's side had worn badly and needed replacing. It was so bad that the mechanic recommended that I purchase one from a used tire place that was just down the street. I agreed.

The next day while a technician was changing the tire, the manager asks if I knew anyone in my church whom might need a new car. I said, "maybe." He pointed to a mid-sized sedan parked out next to the road. I liked the looks of it. He informed me that he bought the car for his wife, but then decided to sell it. The car was about eight years old but still in good condition. It had low mileage and the man promised me that he would put some new tires on it if I would buy it. And after asking some questions, doing a little investigating, and praying, I did just that. A car dealer in my church told me that I got a very good deal. It was certainly the hand of the Lord at work to meet our need.

The church honored me a few Sunday's later with a very generous love offering. It was more than enough to pay off the car that I had purchased. In fact, the church was so generous in giving that, in addition to the car, we were able to install some gutters on the front and back of our home and buy a new "Nook" tablet for my wife. (The pastor's wife needs appreciation too!) God's people united in giving and made a tremendous difference. By faith, they all prayed, gave sacrificially, and trusted God to intervene and work a miracle.

Teamwork is the way

Teamwork is the way we achieve God's purpose in the world. It takes the whole church. The Great Commission is the will of God for every follower of Christ. There should be no spectators in the church when it comes to making disciples. Every member of the Body of Christ should be equipped and engage in disciple-making. We must trust in God and give our best. He will intervene in the lives of His children who desire to obey Him and do His will. By God's grace, the Great Commission can be done if all the members of the Body of Christ will pray, give, and work together to achieve it.

The Great Commission is the task of the church to make disciples of all nations as commanded by the Lord Jesus (Matt 28:18-20; Acts 1:8). It looked impossible for those early followers of Christ. How could such a small group of believers get the gospel of Jesus to every person in the known world? The printing press had not yet been invented. They had no gospel tracts to pass out or leave at someone's door. Travel across land was at best by horse, camel, or donkey. Air travel was unthinkable. They had no radio or television. They had no cell phones, in fact they had no phones at all. The believers could not call, text, tweet, or e-mail one another. The apostles, including Paul, had none of the tools we have in the twenty-first century, but they managed to get the gospel to every part of the known world in their day. They trusted God to empower them to do His will. The Great Commission is impossible for man alone, but with God all things are possible (Matt 19:26; Mk 9:23, 10:27; Lk 18:27).

Jesus taught His disciples how the mission would be carried out. They would accomplish it together by God's grace. Every disciple would participate. They would go preaching the gospel in the power of the Holy Spirit and simply trust God to save the lost and transform them. The heavenly strategy to reach the unsaved masses included (1) devoted prayer, (2) divine power, (3) dutiful proclamation, and (4) making disciples by nurturing new believers in the Word of God. The disciples would help the new converts to grow spiritually and then send them out into the world to make even more disciples until all the people groups of the world heard the gospel (Matt 28:18-20; Acts 1:8). The church today must operate by these basic Biblical principles of church growth. New methods may be included, but no principle of Scripture should be denied. God is honored when His people do His work according to His Word and to His glory.

Devoted Prayer

The Great Commission church must first be devoted to prayer. After watching Jesus ascend through the clouds into heaven, the disciples returned from the Mount of Olives to the city of Jerusalem (see Acts 1:9-12). They immediately made their way up into the upper room for the purpose of prayer (vv.13-14). They prayerfully waited for the Holy Spirit's arrival just as the Lord had instructed them. After many days of crying out to God, the promised Holy Spirit came in power (Acts 2:1-2).

Devoted prayer resulted in power for proclaiming the gospel. This is a principle of prayer for the local church: *Waiting in unified prayer leads to the empowerment of the Spirit.*[27] The people of God ought to spend quality time in prayer before they engage in mission. The purpose of such devoted prayer is not to have a day of Pentecost all over again, but to surrender the human will to the will of God and to express the need of the church to depend upon Him and His power to fulfil the Great Commission.

From the account of this prayer gathering in Acts 1:12-26, the Bible reveals five principles for a dynamic prayer cell. The local Great Commission church should assemble, agree, abide, and anticipate a great movement from God in answer to fervent prayer. Once they have heard from God they should take the appropriate action.

1. The church should assemble for Prayer.

The disciples made a choice to get together and pray. All of the apostles (with the exception of Judas Iscariot), the half-brothers of Jesus, along with many men, women, and children assembled in the upper room and prayed together (Acts 1:12-14). In obedience to the Lord's command to wait in Jerusalem, there was no better way to prepare their hearts for that monumental movement and arrival of the Holy Spirit on the Day of Pentecost.

The urgent need for united prayer remains. Church leaders and laity, men and women, boys and girls should assemble and call on God together. Any individual who knows the Lord can pray alone and certainly be heard, but in times of great need the body of Christ should come together for the purpose of prayer.

2. The church should agree in Prayer.

The waiting saints not only assembled to pray but they were in full agreement. The church prayed in "one accord" or with "one mind" (Acts 1:14). The word pertains to a community acting as one.[28] The church was unified in heart and in mind. There was no division in the Body. This is a true check point for prayer among God's people. Are the saints genuinely unified in prayer? Are there any divisions among them (1 Cor 1:10)? Are they walking in love which bonds them together (Col 3:14)? God is very pleased when the brethren "dwell together in unity" (Psalm 133:1).

3. The Church should abide in Prayer.

They made their way back to Jerusalem and into the upper room remained in prayer until the Promise from Heaven came down. When the Day of Pentecost arrived they were still all together in that same place of prayer (Acts 2:1). For about ten days they prayed until the power of the Spirit came upon them and empowered them to take the gospel to the ends of the earth.

4. The Church should anticipate answers to Prayer.

The believers remained in prayer and claimed the promise that Jesus had made to them that the Holy Spirit would come. Jesus had taught them to pray and believe (Matt 21:22). They prayed in faith and anticipated an answer from heaven. The Spirit came upon them like a mighty rushing wind (Acts 2:1-13). It was in the power of the Holy Spirit that the disciples of Jesus set out to complete the daunting task of the Great Commission.

5. The Church should take action after prayer.

God will often give direction during a corporate prayer gathering. Peter must have been meditating on the Word, because he concluded that God wanted to fill the leadership position vacated by Judas Iscariot who betrayed Jesus and later committed suicide (Acts 1:15-20).The disciples had to choose between two men: Joseph called Barsabas and Matthias (Acts 1:23). After another period of prayer for God's guidance and will to be done in the matter they made their selection by casting lots (Acts 1:24-26). The lot favored Mathias and he was added to the role of apostleship (Acts 1:23-24).

Even when assembled saints are seeking the Lord about other matters, God may surface something that needs to be done in preparation for the answer to those prayers. Devoted followers should always be ready to hear from God and be willing to do whatever He desires. God wanted the new apostle in place before the Spirit's descent from heaven. The church had to take action in order to prepare for that historic event of the power of God coming upon them on the Day of Pentecost.

Divine Power

The Great Commission Church must depend on the power of God to reach the world for Christ. God's will cannot be done in man's own strength. The Lord instructed His disciples to wait in Jerusalem until the Spirit came to empower them (see Luke 24:49; Acts 1:4). In Acts 1:8, "power" (*dunamis*) is the same word used of the miracles of Jesus in the New Testament.[29] God's miracle working power, by the presence of the Holy Spirit, is now "upon" His Children for the purpose of completing the Great Commission (Luke 24:49b).

The work and will of God can only be accomplished in the power of God. The Holy Spirit came to reside within those followers of Jesus on this particular day of Pentecost (Acts 2:1-4). All who place their faith in Jesus are sealed by the Spirit (Eph 1:13-14). Believers must be sure to be filled with the Holy Spirit (Eph 5:18, see chp. 10 for more on the power of the Spirit).

Dutiful Proclamation

God's Holy Spirit empowers His children for the purpose of proclaiming the gospel. It is the responsibility of every believer to spread the good news. Jesus said that the disciples "shall be witnesses" (1:8b). Not everyone is called to preach the gospel to congregations, but every believer should be sharing their faith. I have learned three simple steps from the New Testament to help me tell others about Jesus. I begin with a *conversation*, then make a *presentation* of the gospel, and conclude with an *invitation* for the lost person to be saved.

1. Begin a Conversation

Personal evangelism *begins with a conversation*. I have observed that people who are born-again and consider themselves to be great "conversationalists" are often gifted in personal evangelism. Even folks who consider themselves to be shy often speak with others daily about many subjects. People talk about the weather. People talk about sports. People talk about politics. People just talk. Christians talk too. Any Christian who can engage in a conversation can share the gospel.

Jesus had many personal conversations with lost people. He spoke with the woman at Jacob's well by asking her for a drink of water (John 4:7). After her accusers went away one by one, another woman who had been caught in adultery heard the good news from Jesus. She believed in the Lord and went on her way "to sin no more" (John 8:11). A wee little man named Zaccheaus, who collected taxes and extorted people, was called out of a sycamore tree by our Lord. Jesus invited Himself over to the home of Zaccheaus to share and explain the way of salvation (Lk 19:1-10). Jesus also talked with a rich young ruler about eternal life. This man went away sad because he loved his riches more than God (Lk 18:23). A religious man named Nicodemus made his way to Jesus after dark to question Him about some spiritual matters and the great works of God that He was performing (John 3:1-16). Some parents brought their children to Jesus for a blessing and He took time to listen to them and speak to them. He took them in His lap, hugged them, prayed for them, and blessed them. He loved being with children and they loved Him (Matt 19:13-15). Jesus even had a conversation with two condemned criminals as they were being crucified (Lk 23:43).

Jesus got personal with sinners. He loved them. He reached out to them. He was not afraid to be seen with them. Jesus knew that it was not the healthy that needed a physician but those who were sick (Matt 9:12). The lost and oppressed needed the good news and Jesus gave it to them personally. Talk with lost people. Jesus did.

2. Share a Gospel Presentation

Each conversation can lead to a presentation of the gospel truth. Jesus began conversations with many different people in many ways and about many subjects. No matter how the verbal exchange began, it always moved into spiritual matters. Jesus seemed to intentionally turn each conversation in the direction of making a good news presentation. Each evangelistic presentation of Jesus in the New Testament was unique. He always spoke the truth in love and pointed people to faith in Himself, but he did not have a "canned" speech that he delivered every time He encountered a lost person. The presentations of Jesus were personal and suited to each person with whom He conversed.

Jesus always knew what to say to sinners. The woman at the well heard about "living water"(John 4). Nicodemus discovered that a man must be "born again" to enter the kingdom of heaven (John 3:1-16). Jesus told the rich young ruler to sell all of his possessions and give to the poor because He knew that this man's love of money was keeping him from the kingdom (Lk 18:18-23). Jesus visited with Zaccheaus in his home and evidently spent hours talking with him. Perhaps, the tax collector had lots of questions. It takes longer with some than it does others (Lk 19:1-10). One of those thieves dying on a cross alongside Jesus believed on the Lord and found that he would soon be with Him in paradise (Lk 23:43).

Jesus was always personal, and He always presented the truth to sinners in a way that they could understand, repent, and believe. The Holy Spirit will give us speech and help us present the gospel in an understanding way as we converse with lost people (Lk 12:11-12). Let us keep presenting the gospel to people whom we encounter each day as God gives us opportunity (Col 4:2-5). Some lost soul may be saved today. Are you willing to share the gospel?

3. Give an Invitation

Jesus revealed who He was to sinners and then invited them to follow Him. A lost person can be saved in any place and at any time. Ask them to pray with you and receive Jesus Christ as their Lord and Savior by faith. Let us each day get into conversations, make a loving gospel presentation, and give lost souls a personal invitation to trust in Christ for forgiveness of sins and eternal life. Jesus gives an invitation to all the world to come to Him: "Come to me all you who labor and are heavy laden, and I will give you rest. Take my yolk upon you and learn from Me, for I am gentle and lowly in heart, and you will find rest for your souls. For My yolk is easy and My burden is light"
(Matthew 11:28-30).

While writing this chapter, an unfamiliar man dropped by my office seeking some assistance. I invited him inside. In conversation about his need, I began to share with him how Jesus the Son of God watches over His own and meets their needs (Phil 4:19). I shared the gospel with him and asked him if he would kneel with me and trust Christ to be his Lord and Savior. He did. The entire conversation lasted about twenty minutes.

Opportunities to share the gospel may come daily (Col 4:2-4). Let us seize them and win the lost to Christ. Many unsaved people are waiting on someone to tell them the story of Jesus. Will you lead another to Christ today?

Disciple-Making

Jesus instructed His disciples to go into all the world and "make disciples" (Matt 28:19a). God wants more than decisions. He wants disciples! Becoming a disciple is a *process of spiritual growth* that begins at conversion. New believers are baptized and then schooled in the teachings of Jesus and in the whole counsel of the Word of God (Matt 28:19b-20). It requires some hands-on activity. Leading persons to trust in Christ produces converts, but it takes a life-time of spiritual learning and application to fully mature as disciples. Learning should be continuous. The goal is to equip new Christians so well that they themselves become disciple-makers.

The early church did not leave new believers unattended but nurtured them. They spent time together and taught the Word to aid the spiritual growth and development of those who were saved and joining the local church each day (Acts 2:47b). The early church took the responsibility of disciple-making very seriously. They engaged in six purposes. In Acts 2:42-47, the text reveals these six great purposes of the Church that were being implemented:

- Worship
- Evangelism
- Equipping (teaching)
- Ministry (service)
- Fellowship
- Prayer

In his book, *Discipled Warriors*, Chuck Lawless contends that all six of these purposes are crucial to the spiritual health of the local church: "The healthy church builds on its solid biblical and theological foundation to make disciples. Disciple-making bodies teach their members all that Jesus commanded. They teach the purposes of the church. They guide in learning to worship. They teach how to serve, evangelize, pray, equip, and fellowship. They help believers apply and evaluate this faith in every area of their lives."[30]

These six purposes will be priorities in a spiritually healthy church. Devoted disciples will participate in worship, evangelism, teaching, serving, and praying as they connect in fellowship. All of the interaction, programs, and activities of believers should include one or more of these six purposes. All things should be done for "edification" (1 Cor 14:26). Believers who gather to build one another up in love will mature into Christ-likeness and do the will of God (Eph 4:11-16). The local church that is led by a pastor-teacher who equips the saints to employ their spiritual gifts can then serve others to the glory of God (Eph 4:11; 1 Peter 4:10-11). They will be stronger disciples and better prepared to discover and carry out the personal plan that God has for each of them.

Followers of Christ must persevere in Disciple-making until He comes back again and completes our redemption (1 Thess 5:23-24). God calls all of His children to be mature disciples and to make more and more disciples until "the end of the age" (Matt 28:20b). This is God's will for the local church.

For Further Study

Coleman, Robert E. *The Master Plan of Discipleship*. Grand Rapids: Baker Books, 1987.

Klauber, Martin I. and Scott Manetsch. *The Great Commission*. Nashville: Broadman & Holman, 2008.

Lawless, Chuck and Tom S. Rainer. *The Challenge of the Great Commission*. Louisville: Pinnacle Publishers, 2005.

Putman, Jim. *Real-life Discipleship*: Colorado Springs: NavPress, 2010.

CONCLUSION

What does God desire for you to be? God wants you to be a disciple of Jesus Christ (Matt 10:38; 16:24). God's will for you is to seek His face and become more and more like Jesus every day. Keep taking in the Word. Keep praying. Keep telling the story of Jesus and of His love and grace. Just be a disciple. Discipleship leads to discovery.

I have never known a devoted disciple of Jesus Christ who did not eventually find his way and purpose in life. Of course, it is a process and therefore, it takes time. I have learned that it may take lots of time, even a lifetime. But that too is God's will for His children. There is purpose in the process. It is God's will that we keep coming to Him (Matt 7:7). God uses the periods of questioning, the hours of Bible study and prayer, and even the frustrations to shape us into the likeness of His Son. Indeed, He works all things together for this greater purpose (Rom 8:28-29).

If you are still seeking to know God's plan for your life, it is a good thing. It is my prayer that this short work has encouraged you to keep in step with Him. There will be opened and closed doors along the way (Rev 3:7-8). In His time, God who is completely faithful, will show you the way which you should go (Ps 32:8). I am reminded of Paul who tried to go about preaching the gospel in places that needed the truth but God stopped Him (Acts 16:6-7).

The great apostle did not know where God wanted him to go, so he stopped and waited (v.8). Then, in the night, God gave him direction and he was back on track (vv.9-10).

Right now get up and go in the direction that you believe God is leading you. You have prayed. You have studied. You know in your heart what you believe God wants you to do, so get up and get going. If you start in the wrong direction, fear not, somehow God will stop you. He will redirect you. He will get you on the right path. And no matter what, keep walking with the Lord. No matter the costs, be a disciple (Matt 10:37-39). This is God's will for you.

NOTES

1   Boyd Hunt, *Redeemed: Eschatological Redemption and the Kingdom of God* (Nashville: Broadman & Holman Publishers, 1993), 9.
2   W.A. Criswell, "The Scarlet Thread of Redemption." *The Believers Study Bible* (Nashville: Thomas Nelson, 1991), 1835.
3   Wayne Grudem, C. John Collins, and Thomas R. Schreiner, *Understanding the Big Picture of the Bible* (Wheaton: Crossway, 2012), 8.
4   Curtis Vaughan, *The Letter to the Ephesians* (Nashville: Convention Press, 1963), 48.
5   Ralf Earl, *1 & 2 Timothy*, The Expositors Bible Commentary, vol 11 (Grand Rapids: Zondervan, 1981), 358.
6   D. Michael Martin, *1 & 2 Thessalonians*, The New American Commentary, vol 33 (Nashville: Broadman & Holman Publishers, 1995), 188.
7   David L. Allen, *Hebrews*, The New American Commentary, vol 35 (Nashville: Broadman and Holman Publishing, 2010), 574.
8   Ibid..
9   Timothy George, *Galatians*, The New American Commentary, vol 30 (Nashville: Broadman & Holman Publishing, 1994), 396.
10 Dietrich Bonhoeffer, *The Cost of Discipleship* (New York: Macmillian Publishing, 1963), 99.
11 D.Micheal Martin, *First Thessalonians,* The New American Commentary, vol 33 (Nashville:Broadman & Holman Publishers, 2004), 181.
12 Elizabeth Elliott, *God's Guidance* (Grand Rapids: Revell, 1997), 99
13 Tim LaHaye, Finding the Will in a Crazy Mixed-Up World (Grand Rapids: Zondervan, 1989), 100.
14 Leon Morris, *Hebrews,* The Expositors Bible Commentary, vol 12 (Grand Rapids: Zondervan, 1981), 113
15 David L. Allen, *Hebrews,* The New American Commentary, vol 35 (Nashville: Broadman & Holman, 2010), 543

16 Billy Graham, *Hope for the Troubled Heart,* (Dallas: Word Publishing, 1991), 53.

17 Merrill C. Tenney, *John,* The Expositors Bible Commentary, vol 9 (Grand Rapids: Zondervan, 1981), 146.

18 Curtis Vaughan, *The Letter to the Ephesians* (Nashville: Convention Press, 1963), 111.

19 John MacArthur, *Ephesians,* (Chicago: Moody Press, 1986), 248.

20 Ibid., 249.

21 Jerry Vines, *Spirit Life* (Nashville: Broadman & Holman, 1998), 102.

22 Wayne Grudem, *1 Peter,* Tyndale New Testament Commentaries, vol 17 (Grand Rapids: Eerdmans, 1990), 175.

23 Thomas R. Schreiner, *1, 2 Peter, Jude,* The New American Commentary, vol 37 (Nashville: Broadman & Holman, 2003), 214.

24 Ibid., 215

25 Warren Wiersbe, *1 Peter,* The Bible Exposition Commentary, vol 2 (Wheaton: Victor Books, 1989), 423.

26 Billy Graham, *The Holy Spirit* (Dallas: Word Publishing, 1988), 137.

27 John B. Polhill, *Acts.* The New American Commentary (Nashville: Broadman and Holman, 1992), 90.

28 Darrell L. Bock, *Acts* (Grand Rapids: Baker Academic, 2007), 78.

29 Polhill, 85.

30 Chuck Lawless, *Disciple Warriors* (Grand Rapids: Kregal Publications, 2002), 47.

Steak, shrimp, Baked potato, salad - Bread
mushrooms + mixed vegetables -

you are a hater ~~Hate redefined to discredit Christians~~ if you believe th
Bible. If you are a patriot, not a socialist,
freedom of speach, true feminism, capitalism
not communism, integrity vs ends justify
means, Truth vs propaganda (relativity),
Evil vs good Justice vs political + social
justice, importance of hereafter vs Here + Now
God vs State, Conservative vs Liberal (Liberals
aren't called bad names they are perfect)
That equality "all men are created equally" means
equality of opportunity not of results God distributes
his resources, man not to redistribute others success.

The foolishness of ~~thinking~~ attempting to
change society by name calling, as if
it makes you superior. you read her in
comparison to Krant, Smil, willy and you
are embarassed for her ~~bandishment~~ lack of
honesty & modesty.
What is missing is hate's opposite love.
Have you noticed how they talk freely about hate,
an emotion that undergirds their politics, but
seldom on love - we tend to talk about what
we are occupied with, either good or ~~bad~~ evil
hate or love.

CPSIA information can be obtained at www.ICGtesting.com
Printed in the USA
LVOW08s1807190714
395113LV00002B/2/P

9 781462 738328